"A Guide for Pastors, Leaders, and Congregations."

How to Grow a Congregation Spiritually and in Number through Preaching

by

Dr. Clinton Craig Hoggard

DORRANCE
PUBLISHING CO
EST. 1920
PITTSBURGH, PENNSYLVANIA 15238

Dorrance Publishing Co
585 Alpha Drive
Pittsburgh, PA 15238
Visit our website at *www.dorrancebookstore.com*

ISBN: 978-1-6376-4168-2
eSIBN: 978-1-6376-4805-6

Robert Simmons One Photography Philadelphia, Pennsylvania

"A GUIDE FOR PASTORS, LEADERS, AND CONGREGATIONS."

How to Grow a Congregation Spiritually and in Number through Preaching

Problem

Vine Memorial Baptist Church has a serious problem drawing lapsed and new members into the church. The problem stemmed from the history of the church, which was organized by a strong family and the founding pastor. Over the years, the problem became the means by which people were accepted or not accepted into the Vine Memorial family. Over time, many people left the church feeling unappreciated, disrespected, undervalued, and unloved. Unity between the leaders, congregation, and community was low, and Vine Memorial was not seen by the community as a loving church or a church to become a part of. Young people were not participating, some young people left, and it was very difficult to get young people to participate and worship at Vine.

METHOD

In December 2015, a Local Advisory Committee was formed to plan, prepare, and organize a strategy that would create data to address the problem and to create unity among the leaders of the church, the congregation, and the community. Three groups were created to gather such needed information. One group of five persons was comprised of lapsed members, another group of five persons was comprised of prospective new members, and six local pastors who had participated at Vine in various ways over the past 10 years made up the third group. The purpose of the pastors' group was to address the question: Can preaching address the problem of inclusion of lapsed and new members at Vine Memorial Baptist Church?

Conclusions

The study strongly suggests that preaching can impact the problem of drawing lapsed and new members to Vine Memorial. It also shares how preaching and the preacher should interact with the members. Preaching should be simple, should use the language of those in the pew, and should address the needs of all persons hearing the sermon. The study also shares how the preacher must understand who is in the pew and what each person in the pew deals with on a daily basis. And finally, the study may also have implications for other forms of ministerial education.

TABLE OF CONTENTS

    Biblical and Theological Foundations
    Description and Theological Portrait of the Ministry Context for the
    Project
    Research and Evidence of Critical Reflection and Application
    What the Project Entailed
    Initiatives of Implementing the Project

    Impact on the People in the Context of Ministry During and After Project
    Implementation
    Value of the Project for Ministry of the Church
    Insights into Ministry as a Consequence of Implementing the Project
    Project Concerns and Opportunities in the Community
    Congregation and Community Transformation as a Result of Project Im-
    plementation

    Findings and Practices for Ministry

Motivation for Other Ministry Contexts
Where is Vine Memorial Baptist Church in All of This?
Where Does Vine Go from Here?

ACKNOWLEDGEMENTS

A special thank you to the Doctor of Ministry Local Advisory Committee, Chairman Reverend Dr. Arthur R. White (Senior Pastor of Peoples Community Baptist Church, West Philadelphia, Pennsylvania), Deaconess Jackie Wright, and Deacon William Bryant III, Church Secretary, (Vine Memorial Baptist Church, West Philadelphia, Pennsylvania). Thank you also to Reverend Dr. James Sterling Allen, Pastor Emeritus, and to Vine Memorial Baptist Church, West Philadelphia, Pennsylvania. Special thanks to my pastor and mentor Reverend L.S. Williams and his wife the late Clara Williams of Detroit, Michigan, for all their support. Thank you to Reverend George Marshall, Detroit, Michigan. A special thanks to Marvin Smith, Theological & General Services Librarian, Jeron Ashford, Operation Services Manager, and Andrea Reed, Media & Digital Services Librarian at Eastern University, Saint Davids, Pennsylvania, for your support and assistance. To my mother, the late Margaret Hoggard-Winkey, and my father, the late Richard Winkey Sr., thanks for your faithfulness and the teachings of Jesus Christ you instilled in my life. Thank you to my daughter, Margaret Zenobia Hoggard, who showed me patience, though she was just a young child, while I attended seminary in Detroit, Michigan. Thank you to all my brothers and sisters, especially Lottie-Mae, Leroy, Gloria, and Ronald who have gone on to be with the Lord, for all the sermons and church events you faithfully attended with me. Special thanks to my brother, friend, and confidant Reuben A. Hoggard for all your financial and spiritual support. Thank you to my sister Marie Hoggard Smallwood for always lending a listening ear. Thank you to my best friend Reverend

Nathan Coleman and the Bethel Baptist Church of Phoenixville, Pennsylvania, for all your love and support over the years. It is with thankfulness and joy I salute, honor, and appreciate all the hard work, support, dedication, and commitment everyone contributed to my ministry. Without your support, the achievement of the Doctor of Ministry degree would not have been possible. To God be the glory!

INTRODUCTION

There is a great need for Vine Memorial Baptist Church to have better relations with the community in which it sets and serves. I make this statement because one day I was in the grocery store. A young lady recognized me. However, I did not know who she was. She said, "Hello Reverend Hoggard, how are you?"

I said, "I am fine, how are you?"

She told me her name. I began to apologize for not recognizing who she was. She said, "That's all right, I know you have to remember more people than people have to remember you." She went on to tell me how appreciative she was for the kindness, respect, and love I gave to her, embracing her each time she would visit Vine Memorial. She told me how she enjoyed my preaching, how simple it was to follow, how energized and challenging and encouraging it was to hear me preach and pray.

Then she began to tell me how she did not feel that same energy, love, and kindness from other people she would encounter at Sunday School, Bible Study, and Noonday and Evening Prayer Meeting. She told me how discouraging it was, how she did not want to attend Vine anymore. She told me that at times she would come and visit and another Associate Minister was preaching that morning and the sermon was not simple to follow, or encouraging, or empowering. She talked about the importance of Sunday Morning Worship and how it was important for beginning her week on a positive note. She expressed how she needed a good sermon, a good prayer, and good fellowship from her brothers and sisters. She said it was important for her to have a loving church family who valued her gifts, time, and presence. For her, this was not always the case when she would attend Vine. After the conversation, I knew it was important for me to plan, prepare and organize a strong Local Advisory Committee that would understand the needs of the people and how to implement strategies that ensure that this young woman, and others like her, would no longer go away disappointed from Vine Memorial Baptist Church.

Beginning December 2015, each Wednesday from 1:30 to 3:00 pm, the Local Advisory Committee met to plan, prepare, and strategize ways to address the problem that had faced Vine from its inception 85 years previously. The aim of the committee was to educate leadership and the congregation about the importance of being welcoming and loving to all humankind. The problem was addressed through much dialogue, with leadership, the congregation, and community. Training and awareness were also tools used to combat the problem. Ultimately, we interviewed three specific groups, comprised of lapsed members, prospective new members, and local pastors with connections to Vine. Our goal was to answer the question: Could preaching influence the church leadership, congregation, and community to establish a more welcoming church community for lapsed and prospective new members for Vine Memorial Baptist Church?

CHAPTER 1

Biblical and Theological Foundations

The project seeks to identify and understand factors inhibiting the ability of Vine Memorial Baptist Church to bring lapsed members back into Vine and welcome new members into the church. Can preaching move the congregation to be more welcoming to potential members? According to Douglas T. Anderson and Michael J. Coyner, the courage to reach out is central to reconnecting with lapsed members as well as welcoming new members to the church and to Jesus Christ. Anderson shares his experience of running on the track team during his senior year of high school to explain how it taught him the importance of teamwork relative to bringing lapsed and new members to Christ and to the church:

> *Those lessons proved to be valuable not only on the track; they also became a central metaphor for my understanding of ministry. I came to realize many aspects of ministry require a teamwork that is similar to running a relay race in a track meet. This is especially true for the process of assimilating newcomers.*[1]

According to Anderson and Coyner, making new disciples is not a work that can be done alone. The congregation cannot expect the pastor or a few faithful

---

[1] Douglas T. Anderson and Michael J. Coyner, *The Race to Reach Out: Connecting Newcomers to Christ in a New Century* (Nashville, Tennessee: Abington Press, 2004), ix.

1

to do the work while others stand on the sideline. It is teamwork that requires all ministries working together, as God has ordained it to be. An immediate response is necessary when newcomers or lapsed members visit Vine. They say, just as when we are running a race, quickness is crucial. It is also important, when visitors attend Vine, that we contact them immediately. Not doing so could leave the visitors feeling that their visit is not important, not appreciated, and not valued by the congregation.[2]

Timing is an element of importance in seeking to connect newcomers and lapsed members to Vine and to Christ. Timing, urgency, and acts are valuable to moving the visitors into the next stage connecting them to Vine and Christ. When a runner runs, he or she is very aware of the importance of turns on the track. It is important not to fight the turns on the track course, but to flow smoothly into the turns, thus allowing the runner to sustain balance and speed. This is equally important in making disciples, connecting lapsed members, and inviting new members to Christ. Maintain the stride, yet be aware of the changes that come unexpectedly. Make the adjustments required without delay in the process of making new disciples for Christ and Vine.

The runner should be mindful of the importance of handing off the baton smoothly, without disruption or dropping the baton. This is a necessary skill in making the race successful. Likewise, it is important that the church maintain contact with visitors and get important information about their physical and spiritual needs, interests, gifts, talents, and desires. This will enable the various ministries at Vine to connect with the newcomers in many different ways. Consistent practice is necessary for the ministries, leaders, and team to be successful in bringing newcomers and lapsed members to Vine, connecting them to others, and making disciples for Christ.

"Let us run with patience the race that is set before us, looking unto Jesus, the author and finisher of our faith" (Hebrews 12:1-2, KJV). The writer of Hebrews uses an illustration of a race, a common athletic event during Greco Roman times. There are runners and witnesses. These "witnesses" are examples, though they were not "made perfect" (11:40). They trusted God, living for Him to the end. Their testimonies encouraged others to do the same. The writer exhorts his audience (runners) to "strip off" (i.e., take off excess clothing or weights while running) anything that hinders living faithfully, particularly sin (12:1).

---

[2] Anderson, *The Race to Reach Out,* ix -xiv.

Instead of being sidetracked or encumbered, believers should run with endurance by focusing on Christ, the One who founded the Christian faith (12:2) and created a path forward for those to come. He not only started it, but He is the ultimate example. Christ is the one who demonstrates how perfect faith looks when temptation arises to overwhelm us. The writer inspires believers not to become weary and give up (12:3), as one would toward the end of a race. Instead, believers should be motivated by remembering how Christ endured a humiliating, excruciatingly painful death and overcame sin while restoring our relationship with God, which was the joy set before Him (12:2).[3]

Description and Theological Portrait of the Ministry Context for the Project

The theological portrait of the ministry context of Vine cannot be understood without unpacking the early history of the church. Vine Memorial Baptist Church was organized in 1932 in the West Philadelphia home of Mr. & Mrs. Albert Franklin, 137 N. Salford Street, and selected as its first pastor Reverend Dr. Leonard George Carr. Dr. Carr served the church faithfully and effectively for 44 years. The initial location of the Vine Memorial Baptist Church (then Vine Street Baptist Church) was on the second floor of a Lodge Hall located at 57th and Vine Streets. The small congregation worshipped in the Lodge Hall for two years until it was relocated to 56th and Vine Streets. By the year 1945, the congregation had outgrown this location and moved to 56th Street and Girard Avenue. It then changed its name from Vine Street Baptist Church to Vine Memorial Baptist Church.

Under the leadership of Dr. Leonard George Carr, the church became a haven in the community where many came to know Jesus Christ and found refuge in times of crises, be they natural or humanly instigated. Dr. Carr set the tone for the church to be in the community. The church met the community's physical as well as spiritual needs. The church supported social and educational programs as well as established programs of its own that benefited the community.

Vine Memorial Baptist Church has been of great support to groups like Carol Park Community Council, Haddington Leadership Organizations, and charities encouraging to the community. The church created its own credit union, which was designed to assist people in becoming financially independent

---

[3] A. Okechukwu Ogbonnaya, *Precepts for Living 2016-2017: International Sunday-School Lessons, Volume 19*, (Chicago, Illinois: Urban Ministries, 2016), 94.

as well as economically secure. In 1976, the beloved pastor of Vine Memorial Baptist Church was called home to be with the Lord. In 1978, the church, along with the congregation, elected Reverend James S. Allen as its second pastor. For over 37 years, Reverend Allen has stood firmly in the tradition established by Dr. Carr. Serving the community has become the hallmark of Vine Memorial Baptist Church. The church has a pantry ministry, which provides food for the hungry, and a clothing giveaway for those in need of clothing. The church has created a Community Outreach Ministry that participates in voter registration, voter education, and voter participation. Through these ministries, Vine seeks to serve beyond the four walls of the church building.

Although this is a wonderful theological portrait of the church, my past six years serving as an Associate Minister at Vine Memorial have clearly allowed me to experience a breakdown in Vine's ability to connect with lapsed and new members as well as make disciples for Christ. Vine has not always been welcoming to lapsed and new members. Many have said of their experience that if you became a part of the church during the eras of the organizers, Mr. & Mrs. Albert Franklin and Founder/Pastor Reverend Dr. George Carr, you were truly considered a member of Vine Memorial. Others have said, if you were not connected in some way to the founder, organizers, or family members of that era, you were not a true member of Vine. This attitude has created a divide between the community and the congregation, putting a strain on the church's ability to reconnect with lapsed members or invite prospective new members into the life of Vine Memorial. On many occasions, lapsed and new members would join Vine, but as time passed, they would gradually stop participating.

On occasion, it was my pleasure to run into these former members and attenders. The conversations always included the sharing of their feelings of rejection, disconnection, abandonment, disappointment, hurt, and isolation. Many felt they had no value, some felt they were not appreciated, and others felt they were not loved, respected, or included. Many who had talents, gifts, a desire to serve, love, praise, and worship the Lord were left with many questions for God about the institution called Church and Vine Memorial in particular. Many looked to Vine with questions as they sought to be disciples for Christ: Can you help me? Can I trust you? Can we have relationship? These questions were never answered. It is my concern that Vine has become so close and family-centered that it's become insular and self-serving and contributes to the problems that face Vine today.

The groups I interviewed for this project, which consisted of both lapsed and prospective new members (see Appendices K and L), expressed similar responses:

- The congregation is not warm to newcomers.
- There is no consistent follow-up to newcomers visiting.
- Youth participation is scarce to non-existent.
- The pastor is a good preacher, but sometimes I do not resonate with his language.

Participants were asked other questions about why they used to attend church and why they no longer attend (see Appendix M, Evangelical Church Shopping Explained). What they said, as well as what they did not say, was alarming. Examples include: I was not fed by the preacher, I did not get anything out of the sermon, and the pastor seemed to talk at me instead of talk to me. The sermon did not speak to my situation. What I really heard them saying was, "I did not feel personally included in the preaching experience." It was my observation that some of the listeners were focusing on issues that did not allow them to receive the gospel message. Some were listening as slaves to life circumstances: fears, guilt and doubt. According to Gardner C. Taylor:

> *Thus, every preacher ought never forget in his preaching that one preaches to people who are initially and finally solitary animals with their own fears and courage, grief and guilt, joy and sorrow, anxiety and anger, and with that deep age-old hunger which the bread of this world cannot satisfy and a thirst which the waters of this life cannot quench. Jesus asserted this of which I now speak when he said, "Man shall not live by bread alone." This wistful yearning for spiritual reality and experience is expressed in a song my elders sang in the long ago, "I woke up this morning with my mind stayed on Jesus."*[4]

Therefore, the preacher must feel the people and resonate with their life struggles, pains and hurts, fears, and uncertainty in order for the gospel message to

---

[4] Gardner C. Taylor, as quoted in *The Company of Preachers: Wisdom on Preaching, Augustine to the Present*, ed. Richard Lischer (Grand Rapids, Michigan: William B. Eerdmans, 2002), 111.

be transforming to all situations and life circumstances and connect those who are lost to Christ and the church.

Thomas G. Long, the author of *The Witness of Preaching*, says that as preachers, whether we say it or not, we have been connected to these persons in ministry, directly or indirectly. We have served some family member or relative in hospital rooms, been with them in court rooms, and visited them in their homes. We may have spent previous hours in prayer for ourselves and for those who will worship with us. We may have attended church school class or taught a class, listened with care to a person in distress or have been listened to by someone, or met with church leaders around a matter concerning church business. We may have had something to eat or drink or fellowship with persons in the fellowship hall, been given a last-minute announcement to read, or listened to the choir rehearse for an upcoming service or event at the church. Whether we have been praying, interacting, teaching, or simply listening, we have been involved in the lives of the people to whom we will preach. We have moved from the pew to the pulpit.[5.] "What matters," writes Moltmann, "is that public preaching and the preacher should not be isolated from the simple, every day and matter-of-course language of the congregation's faith, the language used by Christians in the world."[6.]

Long's comments summarize my beliefs about the preacher and preaching. As preachers, we should not only speak but should work equally hard to hear and listen to the hurts of those who visit our congregations and to address not only the physical needs but also the spiritual needs of each person we come into contact with. We must understand how we are involved in the struggles of the common people, including those who do not look like us, who don't drive the best cars, eat the best foods, live in the finest homes, attend the best schools, or even have little to no education. We must understand our own struggles against the principalities and powers in our faithfulness and through our sinful obedience to the evil forces of the world. As we share the text, we must do so through these lenses and bear the truth of the gospel to all humankind. When we understand who sits in the pews, we will be more prepared to speak to the situations of all persons visiting, as well as those who are a part of the congregation. The participants in my interviews, along with author Marshall Shelly, make it clear that all preaching is unique in that all preachers come

---

[5.] Thomas G. Long, *The Witness of Preaching*, (Louisville: Westminster John Knox Press, 2005), 3-4.
[6.] Jürgen Moltmann, as quoted in Long, *The Witness of Preaching*, 4.

with distinct and individual personalities. In order for preaching to make a difference in the lives of those to whom we preach, "preachers must preach in spite of themselves instead of preaching because of themselves."[7]

The preached message must be a part of the preacher's life. There must be something and someone greater than the preacher that sustains the message and frames and shapes the message in a way that the hearer can be transformed beyond his/her situation. Through preaching, God wants the preacher to be a witness. The Apostles knew this: "For we cannot help speaking about what we have seen and heard" (Acts 4:20, NIV). This was part of Paul's commission: "You will be his witness to all men of what you have seen and heard" (Acts 22:15, NIV). The preacher must stand strong and hold strongly to what God has given him/her in order to bear witness to Christ. This solidifies the message that God has given and allows the preacher to own the message. The message is authentic and holds transforming power for those who receive it. As Shelley says:

> *Preaching is not what we do; it is what we are. When God wants to make a preacher, he has to make that person, because the work we do cannot be isolated from the life we live. God prepares the person for the work and the work for the person, and if we permit Him, he brings them together in his providence. God knows us better than we know ourselves. He'd never put us into a ministry where he could not build us and use us.*[8]

Preaching is at its best when the preacher incorporates into the message the goodness of Christ, brings encouragement and hope, builds godliness, and brings resolution. This can also be helpful in bringing back lapsed members into Vine and welcoming new members to Christ. Shelley shares the following insights:

> *The negative often focuses on what people and Satan do. The positive focuses on God's answer, God's glory, God's nature, God's salvation. God wants people to experience hope, peace, acceptance, courage. Bad news makes people feel bad. So while the negative is useful, it is rarely helpful to leave that as the last word. People need not only stop sinning, but also to start doing God's*

---

[7] Marshall Shelley, *Changing Lives Through Preaching and Worship* (NY: Random House, Inc., 1995).
[8] Shelley, *Changing Lives*, 13.

will. Preaching is both destructive and constructive, tearing down what's wrong and building what's right. Preaching positively encourages people to do what's right. Sermons often have greater emotional impact when we begin with the negative, show the need, and then bring resolution by showing what God can do.[9]

Long says that greater than membership is unity, which serves as the connecting bond, the indwelling of the Holy Spirit. If the Church consists of those who are united to Christ and are members of His body, it is evident that the bond that unites them to Christ also unites them to each other. The bond between Christ and His body is the Holy Spirit, which He gives to dwell in all that are united to Him by faith. By one spirit we are baptized into one body, for we are partakers of that one Spirit. The Holy Spirit is the spirit of love as well as of truth; therefore, all those in whom He dwells are one in affection as well as faith. They have the same inward experience, the same conviction of sin, and the same repentance toward God and faith in our Lord Jesus Christ. They have the same love of holiness, and desire for conformity to the image of God. There is, therefore, an inward fellowship or genuine relationship between them, which proves them to be one spirit.[10]

Christ dwells by His Spirit in all His members, and thus unites them as one living whole, leading all to believe the same truths, and connecting all in the bond of peace. This is the unity of which the Apostle speaks in Ephesians 4:4. Greater than membership is holiness. Holiness makes the church a living body, and therefore is its source of growth and spiritual maturity. God, the Holy Spirit, is the author of its growth. "You are all sons and daughters of God through faith in Christ Jesus, for all of us who were baptized into Christ have clothed ourselves with Christ" (Galatians 3:26 -28).

God is the source and origin of all power, and His power is available as a source of blessings. He seeks to express and to extend His power through humankind, who is made in His image and likeness. He is the resource and regenerator. Humankind, in co-operation with God and Christ, has the potential to be the expression, the expansion and the extension of God's power. [11]

---

[9] Ibid., 48-50.
[10] Long, *The Witness of Preaching,* 15-51.
[11] Ronald O. Brown, *in Preaching with Power: Sermons by Black Preachers*, ed. Joe Aldred (London: Cassel, 1998), p. 71.

Acts 1:1 says, "Jesus began both to do and teach." The Holy Spirit is helping us to be shaped into the model that Christ wants us to be. He is interceding for us in our prayers and in our groaning that cannot be uttered. He is renewing and He is improving us every day. In 2 Corinthians 3:18, the Bible says, "And we all, with unveiled face beholding the glory of the Lord, are being changed into his likeness from one degree of glory to another."

We have the potential at Vine Memorial Baptist to succeed both as a church and as individuals. I would like to ask these questions to the members of Vine: How do you see your church in five years? Are you satisfied with the spiritual growth and development of your church? Are you satisfied with the quality of worship? Who is your neighbor? Are your neighbors only those you like? Are your neighbors only your family and friends? Are your neighbors only those who are connected to the organizers and founders of the Church? Or are your neighbors the poor and marginal and those who have no voice? Who is your neighbor, Vine?

The way of the Church is not easy, but its struggles and its tribulations, its persistence and its trust can all be seen in the context of God's promise of certain victory. By the power of the risen Lord, she is given strength to overcome patiently and lovingly the afflictions and hardships which assail her from within and without, and to show forth in the world the mystery of the Lord until at last it will be revealed in total splendor.[12.]

The story of Nehemiah begins with a concern. Here we see Nehemiah locked in slavery and servitude in a foreign land, in exile, and yet his thoughts are not for himself, nor for his personal condition. Instead, his thoughts are for his people; these people who God loves, not simply because they are "the people of God" but because they are Nehemiah's people who are a part of him. So, we should not be worried about what we will eat, or what we will wear, or who will be the next president of the United States of America. I am in no way downplaying the importance of voting or the presidential election of 2016 or our daily human needs. However, I am pressing the point that Nehemiah is primarily concerned for the spiritual well-being of his people. Is the church concerned about inviting and welcoming lapsed members and new members into the church, into personal relationship with Christ? Is your concern simply about the spiritual future of those who have gone astray? Making disciples for Christ? Jesus fully identified with a fallen humanity to the point of incarnation

---

12. Olu A. Abiola, in Aldred, *Preaching with Power*, 38.

9

and death. What are you identifying with, Vine? And what is the cost? We are fully aware that God cannot resist an available person, because God is seeking out the people like David, you, and me, who do not accept the word "impossible." God is seeking people who will stand in the midst of the storm, who will "ride or die" with Him no matter what the cost. I Corinthians 1:27, 29 remind us:

> God chose the foolish things of the world to shame the wise; God chose the weak things of this world to shame the strong. God chose the lowly things that are not to nullify the things that are, so that no one may boast before Him.

If the world thinks you are any of these things, then God is seeking you. Then the question to answer, Vine, is, are you available to God? Are you available to those who are seeking Christ through Vine Memorial Baptist Church?

One of the assignments for the project was to ask 10 interview questions (see Appendix L) regarding concerns around low participation of lapsed members and prospective new members at Vine. The question that was asked by the interviewing committee member to the participants was, did you attend church when you were young, and if so, why? If not, why not? I clearly recall several of the participants indicating how they were interested and enjoyed attending the events at the church, but they had no one to take them. They shared the week-to-week challenge they faced in getting to worship with no support from home. They described how available they were and how they looked forward to participating in church each week. They went on further to share how this made them closer to the church and more available to Christ.

Finally, the participants shared how being available to Christ impacted family members who were living in the home who were not attending church. These family members were convinced, convicted, converted and transformed by the power of the Holy Spirit, and some became members of the church. The participants realized that the lack of family support was not a closed door, and it did not allow them to passively give way to opposition, but, rather, gave them strength to resist opposition. Jesus said, "In this world you will have trouble, and trouble arrives in all shapes and forms." It is important that we understand the experience of opposition is not to be measured or viewed as a closed door, but is to be seen as a means to which we can be more available to God.

Research and Evidence of Critical Reflection and Application

Many of the sources examined for use to present and defend my argument gave great insights into reaching people and helping persons to grow in their faith. Much of the literature speaks to putting methods into place that will connect leaders, congregations, communities, lapsed members, and new members in making and becoming Disciples for Christ. Much of the literature used to defend my argument is drawn from African American preachers and the role and importance of preaching in the African American church context. My argument aims to push that preaching can positively impact low partici-pation of lapsed and prospective new members at Vine Memorial Baptist Church. Although there is information available around the subject of lapsed members and new members, it is from a European perspective. Effective use has been made of such literary sources where possible. In order to stay true to my context, I have chosen to defend my argument using the voices of African American preaching scholars, along with the three interview groups who were the core of my project. This approach provides a truer African American per-spective of my context and substantive support to my project report and dis-sertation. This approach will be very resourceful to my argument, findings, and outcomes. It will further be effective for research ministry moving forward and the future ministry context of Vine Memorial Baptist Church.

Although the data found some concerns about preaching at times, no major link between the preaching at Vine and the low level of participation among lapsed and prospective new members was found. However, the project finds preaching to be a core element and most important in drawing in and growing the faith of lapsed and prospective new members to Vine. Therefore, preaching must have specific and particular elements that open the door to the Holy Spirit to transform lives and shape the identity of leadership, the con-gregation and the community. The gospel message must be delivered with en-ergy, conviction, power, and confidence. It must also speak to the situations facing all people who hear the Word of the Lord. The aim of the preachers who have been chosen to speak to my argument can be best summed up in the words of Joe Aldred:

> *Preaching is taken seriously by Black Christians everywhere as the primary means by which the Gospel is communicated ... Black preachers are at work, expounding the Gospel to whoever will listen. Understanding the Gospel as*

the power of God unto salvation, liberty and freedom, they preach with the urgency of "a dying man unto a dying world.[13.]

The Local Advisory Committee spent hours talking about issues we experienced at Vine and concerns and problems we gleaned from the congregation and the community. We talked about the church history, problems that had arisen, and problems that were resolved. We talked about concerns that were not addressed and concerns that were resolved. Members of the committee were assigned to interview members of the congregation and the community. The committee took seriously my concerns about Vine Memorial Baptist Church. I diligently searched the work of scholars who have investigated and written on the subject of lack of church participation and the issues involved in drawing lapsed members and new members into the church. I researched African American preaching scholars to see if preaching could be instrumental in addressing this issue at Vine. I explored African American scholarship to support my belief that preaching is essential to making disciples for Christ and spiritually growing the church. The committee interviewed members of Vine Memorial Baptist Church to recruit lapsed family members and prospective new members.

I talked to the Pastor and other Associate Ministers of the Vine Memorial Baptist Church about concerns facing Vine. Many conversations were had with ministry leaders, lay leaders, and members of the congregation. Local Advisory Committee members talked with lay leaders of the congregation and leaders in the community. The committee and I interviewed six African American pastors who have interacted with Vine over the past 10 years by preaching and conducting leadership workshops, special services, and events. These pastors were able to provide insight into the concerns facing Vine. When I lectured, preached, taught Sunday School and Wednesday Morning and Evening Bible Classes, led the New Members Class, conducted workshops, and just had conversation, I was careful to integrate the concerns of low participation of lapsed members and prospective new members. Along with the Local Advisory Committee, I engaged the congregation and community. The outcome provided positive feedback. Many persons saw a great need for the work and committed to be helpful in any way.

[13.] Aldred, *Preaching with Power*, vii.

What the Project Entailed

The project identified lapsed members and prospective new members and their contact information. Each individual person received a phone call, text message, or email. A date, time, and place were scheduled for orientation. Each participate received a reminder letter, text, email, or phone call outlining the time length as well as the specifics of the orientation. Orientation took place for one hour, light refreshments were served, and specific expectations were given to the participants. Consent forms were signed by each participant— one for the participants and one for the Local Advisory Committee records (see Appendix I). A thank you letter was sent to each participant thanking him/her for participating in the project (see Appendix H). Each participant was informed of the date, time, and place for the 10 interview questions (see Appendix L). The questions were presented to collect data from lapsed members and prospective new members as to why they were no longer participants at Vine Memorial Baptist Church. The collected data was used for the purpose of writing the project report.

Planning for the Doctor of Ministry Project began in December of 2015. The Local Advisory Committee was comprised of Clinton Hoggard, Deaconess Jackie Wright, and Deacon William Bryant III, Church Clerk, all of Vine Memorial Baptist Church. The committee was chaired by the Reverend Dr. Arthur R. White, Senior Pastor of People's Community Baptist Church, located in West Philadelphia, Pennsylvania. The context was Vine Memorial Baptist Church, also located in West Philadelphia, Pennsylvania. The Senior Pastor at that time was Reverend Dr. James Sterling Allen, now Pastor Emeritus as of January 1, 2016.

Each week, the Local Advisory Committee met to plan, prepare, and strategize for implementation of the project. The weekly meetings included scheduling dates, times, and places for orientation with lapsed and prospective new members. Interviews with these people would provide data for writing the project report. The 10 interview questions centered around two general aims: 1) to identify reasons for the interviewees' lack of church involvement, and 2) to explore the role of preaching in the church experiences of the interviewees. Each week, the Local Advisory Committee would be given assignments: drafting questions for interviews, drafting thank you letters, and drafting invitations to include dates, times, and locations. The Local Advisory Committee was trained using the procedures prescribed in the Drew Theological Seminary Manual for conducting interviews pertaining to the Doctor of Ministry Project.

The purpose of the proposed research is to address the particular needs of Vine Memorial Baptist Church. The research will attempt to discover why lapsed member participation is low at Vine and why new members are not being welcomed. The research will also attempt to see how preaching can alleviate the problem at Vine. The research will be published in 2017 as a dissertation for the Doctor of Ministry degree in a joint effort with Drew Theological Seminary in Madison, New Jersey.

The participants were divided into two groups. Group one was composed of five adult persons who used to attend Vine Memorial. Group two included five adult persons who do not currently attend Vine Memorial but may be interested in becoming new members. The small size of the groups allows participants to share their stories, perspectives, and experiences, with the hope of revealing their reasons for not currently attending Vine.

A third group, which included six pastors who have interacted through various activities with Vine Memorial over the past 10 years, was also assembled in order to assist the Local Advisory Committee in finding new ways to address the problems of outreach and membership at Vine.

The participants were recruited by me and the research investigation team through families of Vine Memorial Baptist Church. The research was conducted at Vine Memorial Baptist Church in Philadelphia, Pennsylvania. The project exercised transparency and encouraged honesty from all participants involved in the research project as set out by the Institutional Review Board of Drew University, me, and the Local Advisory Committee. The project's aim was to discover problems and explore avenues that can foster change and growth and also lead to further studies of the topic. The data was kept in a secure place while the information was gathered and processed.

Personal names and identities were not divulged to anyone other than the research investigators: Deaconess Jackie Wright, Deacon William Bryant III, and me. Once gathered and analyzed, the collected information was destroyed. All participants were provided a debriefing form. The debriefing form detailed the project's purpose, explained who would take part and what would take place in the project, and detailed what was expected of all participants. Contact information was made available to each participant.

All participants agreed to take part in orientation. The interviews themselves were audio-recorded by the research investigators. Participants were asked 10 questions that were related to their church experiences. All participants were asked to be open, honest, and truthful in their responses. This was helpful to the writing process.

The purpose in recording the information was to allow the candidate to clearly listen to the data for accurate writing of the dissertation. Participants could answer any or all questions but were not required to do so. Participants could end participation in the research process at any time without consequences. Participants were asked to sign and date Ministry Consent Forms. One copy was given to the participant for his/her records and one copy was kept for the Local Advisory Committee. After all 10 questions were asked, participants were welcome to leave. The teamwork by the Local Advisory Committee laid solid ground work for writing the dissertation and for moving forward in future ministry context for Vine Memorial.

Initiatives of Implementing the Project

Implementing the project energized me, and I took the lead in addressing the concerns that face Vine Memorial Baptist Church. Preaching, teaching, and conducting workshops or lectures were done with solid preparation, sensitivity, confidence and care. I presented to the congregation, the community, and the church leadership the issues concerning Vine. I developed relationships with all participants involved and tried to maintain an attitude of kindness, respect, patience, and diligence.

The Local Advisory Committee was trained using the information provided in the Doctor of Ministry Program Manual of Drew University. I strove to include the committee in every aspect of the project, including drafting meaningful questions for the participant groups and making sure materials for the project were provided and available for use. When I gave assignments, I made sure each person clearly understood his/her task. I made myself available to assist the team in any way. I was punctual for meetings, and each meeting was effectively run. I made great use of all the committee members, took constructive criticism well, and made the adjustments needed when constructive criticism was provided by committee members. I attended to any problem that arose while implementing the project. No problem was too big or too small. I feel that I got the best out of all the committee members, while motivating, modeling, and mentoring them with excellence.

I shared with the Committee the goals of the prospectus. Each week, a meeting was held to plan, prepare, and implement the project. The Belmont

Report addressed the following areas in section C: 1) Informed Consent, 2) The Assets & Risks of Research, and 3) The Selections of Subjects. I provided the Local Advisory Committee Members with interview tips but maintained control of the overall project, taking the lead in working with the congregation, church leaders, Chairman of the Deacon Board, deaconesses, deacons, Sunday School, and past and current superintendents. The path through which we achieved the project goals included Wednesday Noonday and Evening Bible Classes and Prayer Meeting Services, New Members Classes, Workshops, Seminars, and Men's Day preaching/lecturing. I have fulfilled the project specifications and identified the problems facing Vine Memorial Baptist Church. Recommendations were presented to leadership for spiritual growth and new insights for future ministry for the congregation, for church leadership, and the community.

CHAPTER 2

Impact on the People in the Context of Ministry During and After Project Implementation

During the project the congregation was energized and enthused to move forward. After the announcement of Pastor Allen's retirement, however, the energy and enthusiasm seemed to lessen. Nevertheless, the Local Advisory Committee continued to implement the project, showing the need for the congregation, leadership, and community to understand the importance of the project.

Each time there was an opportunity to talk with members of the congregation, leadership or the community, the project objectives and goals were included in the discussion. Many people from both the congregation and the community were excited because they saw the need for the positive work and change the project would bring. The excitement was wrapped up in the fact that everyone wanted better relationships between the congregation, the leadership, and the community. The community is very aware of the fact that Vine Memorial is not inclusive or inviting to lapsed and new members. The community has a negative perspective and attitude toward Vine. The community sees Vine as a church who welcomes values and fellowship with those who are members of Vine. But do not respect or see value in those who are not a part of Vine, or those who live in the neighborhood surrounding Vine Memorial. Several of the perspective new member's participants spoke extensively about this problem during the project interview discussion. During the discussion, the perspective new members shared their hurts, disappointments, and their anger, and shared how it was damaging to all, both within and outside of the church. Vine, too, is aware of the divide this reputation has on the body of Christ and to the witness of Vine Memorial Baptist Church and its ability to make disciples for Christ. Vine as a congregation has discussed the need to be different and more welcoming to outsiders and have prayed for God to empower the congregation to be more loving to all humankind.

The implementation of the project was a breath of fresh air to all parties involved. Many people were excited and glad to know that there is hope for repairing the divide between leadership, the congregation, and the community. The implementation of the project received great reviews. People became more transparent, authentic, open, and honest about the concerns that have haunted Vine for many years. Persons began to share their narratives and stories relative to their relationships with Vine. This gave a deeper understanding about the concerns that confront Vine. Members would share with me the deep feelings they had about Vine that they had never shared before. Many expressed a sense of peace that they never experienced before the implementation of the project. The positive feedback was great. Several people still come to me and say, "Who Is your Neighbor?" Many people have become more focused and more committed to being loving and open to those who have come to visit Vine since I preached "Who Is your Neighbor" and challenged Vine to be more loving and inclusive of all people. Vine Associate Ministers rotate preaching while we are seeking a pastor. On this particular Sunday, I preached. People have become intentional and deliberate about the need to receive all people and make everyone feel welcomed, valued, appreciated, and loved at all times. This attitude has become prevalent in homes, in the work place, and in the neighborhoods, as well as among the church family. The work of the project targets leaders, lay leaders, ministers, ministries, the congregation and the community.

The congregation and leadership have become more prayerful. Pastor Allen has encouraged the congregation to pray at 6:00 am, 12:00 noon, 3:00 pm, and 6:00 pm that God would move among the leadership, the congregation, the community, and all people. Each Sunday during pastoral emphasis, Pastor Allen would say, "You see somebody walking down the street, they might be dressed up. But you do not know what kind of burdens they may be carrying, so remember to love one another, be kind to one another. For it is by this they will know we are His children, if we have love; one for the other."

During the project, in December 2015, Pastor Allen announced his retirement one Sunday morning during the Worship Celebration. The congregation was torn by the announcement. Leadership was in transition; what was is no longer. The Senior Pastor is now Pastor Emeritus. The congregation began to grieve, and the weight of losing the Senior Pastor who had served for 30-plus years began to set in. He was only the second of two pastors to serve the church in its 85 years of serving God and the people. The composition of the project now involved an Interim Leadership team. Although these persons were aware of the project, they were not immersed in the project and did not give me the freedom to implement on all levels as Pastor Allen did.

Months ago, in 2015, I was able to share my prospectus at "Super Sunday School General Assembly." The feedback was positive. Persons seemed energized by the prospectus. My teaching, Bible classes, lectures for special events and celebrations, and sermons were prepared around our prospectus: How do we bring back lapsed members to the congregation, and how do we welcome new members into Vine? Can preaching help to accomplish these goals? I recall preaching a sermon the Sunday morning of Friends and Family Day at Vine during implementation of the project. The sermon challenged Vine to answer the question: "Who Is your Neighbor?" Is your neighbor your family? Is your neighbor your friends? Or is your neighbor someone who does not look like you, eat what you eat, live where you live, drive what you drive, dress as well as you dress, or attend some of the finest of colleges and universities? Is your neighbor someone who spitefully uses you? Are these your neighbors too? The feedback from the congregation still resonates today. Those who have heard and were impacted by the sermon continue to come to me and say, "'Who Is My Neighbor?' That was an outstanding sermon—we need more of that."

The project's aim and focus is to get as many people involved in the process as possible for future ministry context growth and development. The Local Advisory Committee listened to as many narratives (stories) as possible, aiming to hear the stories that were never told and to include the people who were rarely or never included. As we listened to all the stories, cries and pleas of leadership, the congregation, the community, it was our desire to see how deep the stories would take us. We sought to hear both what was being said and what was not spoken. Our ears were open; we listened in order to understand, not to be understood. We sought to see where the stories would further lead us. What would the stories tell us that have not been told? How do the stories connect one to the other? How do the stories not connect? How do the stories share common threads? How do the stories speak to the "what is"? And how do the stories speak to "what is to come"? Through the narratives and stories, we sought to see and discover the "what is" and to find outcomes that would be healthy in moving Vine forward in spiritual growth and development and seeking to discover other ministry concerns. We did not only seek the stories of Vine, but we sought to see how the stories of the community connected or failed to connect with the stories of Vine. How in our difference are we all really alike? How can we connect with our own stories as well as the stories of the community? In the narratives of the community and the congregation, we made discoveries that showed us how we are connected to one another. The relationship is like the pastor going from the pew to the pulpit. Until he or she has traveled from the pew to the pulpit, the narratives do not connect the listeners to the gospel message. Until the pastor goes from the pew to the pulpit, the gospel message will not resonate with the congregation or those who hear. Until the pastor cries, like those in the pew, from heartache, pain, disappointment, frustration, brokenness, and sorrow, the pastor cannot preach or reach or resonate with those who are in the pew.

Our narratives and stories connect us one to another. The hymnologist says, "I'll bear another's burden, along the lonely way, or teach that burden bearer with confidence to pray, at home or ever loyal, at home or far away, O blessed Savior, count on me." Until you know one's story, until you bear another's burdens, until you have suffered, hurt and cried like others, you cannot reach or connect with them. One cannot understand or relate to history unless one knows the stories of the past. If you want to know a family, you must know the story of the family. If you want to know a person, you must know the story of the person. Stories are the lifelines to all people, places, and things. Until congregations, leaders, and communities connect their stories to the story of Jesus Christ, we cannot understand another's story. "I love to tell the story of Jesus and his glory, to tell the old, old story, of Jesus and His love." Jesus' love connects us to Him. Jesus' love connects us to His story and the story of Jesus' love connects us to one another. According to Henry Mitchell:

Another imaginative aspect of Black preaching is the choice of illustrations gripping modern parallels to the biblical text. In the process of making a

*point clear, the Black experience is lifted up and celebrated, identity is en-
hanced, and the hearer enters vicariously into the story, making it his or
her story.*[14.]

The project and its involvement of preaching encouraged many sermon topics
given by the ministers of Vine. The sermons were empowering, challenging,
and engaging. The sermons moved many beyond Vine Memorial. Many
shared with me how they were doing ministry in their neighborhoods, communities, and work places, daring to be different and challenging others to do
the same, in ways they had not done before. Although their push for change
lay primarily in Vine, many members began to go beyond Vine.

I recall how aggressively the Local Advisory Committee sought to recruit
both lapsed members as well as prospective new members and how their energy transferred onto leadership and into the congregation. As a result, the
Local Advisory Committee was able to meet its project goals for recruiting
lapsed and new members. The six local ministers who I recruited to participate
in the project (see Appendix E) found the topic to be very much needed. Several of the pastors spoke about the need for more ministry leaders to do something similar with their congregations.

The congregation found the material in the project to be very effective.
The material laid a solid foundation for the congregation and leadership to
build upon. The material was meaningful for change, transformation, spiritual
growth, and moving Vine forward in ministry. Although there were many challenges, a great deal of hope and excitement still lives in the congregation. The
attitude of including only those who were a part of or connected to the founder
and organizers seems to have lessened a bit. Some members have demonstrated
more kindness to visitors and new members.

A few members of the congregation have noticed some progress and
change from how the congregation used to be. The congregation became
more intentional and deliberate about greeting visitors. Each Sunday, the hospitality ministry provided candy in a basket and had greeters at each doorway
entrance to the sanctuary. Also at the entrances to the sanctuary were visitor
comment cards asking visitors two questions: did you feel valued and respected? The many positive responses gave the congregation hope and was a

---

[14.] Henry H. Mitchell, *Black Preaching. The Recovery of a Powerful Art* (Nashville, Tennessee: Abington
Press, 1990), 66-67.

sign of progress and positive small gains. Energy generated within the congregation as a result of the project can be used to create congregational transformation and identity change. Some have said the implementation of the project is greatly needed, and that if we do not own our shortcomings, realize Vine has problems with welcoming outsiders, and do not present the plan to the ministries of Vine Memorial Baptist Church, Vine will not grow. Others have commented, "Where have you been all this time? Keep up the good work you are doing. We need this project and this work." Vine Memorial Baptist Church Deacons, Deaconesses, preachers, other leaders have also responded favorably during discussions about the project.

The congregation has been made aware of the importance of the project as a result of my preaching, teaching, lecturing, presenting workshops/seminars, and one-on-one conversations. Many in the congregation expressed amazement about the fact that their thoughts, views, ideas, and feelings mattered. The congregation was happy about how they could be honest, open, and transparent in answering the questions without repudiation from the committee members. Many shared how the project challenged them to look at views and feelings they harbored against the church, the leadership, and also the community. Congregants expressed the need to be more understanding and relational with the community and with God.

Not all congregants have been as positive and energetic, however. After the announcement of Pastor Allen's retirement, I noticed a decrease in energy and a lack of enthusiasm to move forward. A portion of the congregation has not recovered from this setback, and it has been a challenging time for the entire congregation. The Chairman of the Deacon Board and the Deacons are now the Interim Leadership of Vine Memorial Baptist Church.

During Pastor Allen's leadership, access to the congregation and ministries was more readily available to me. Persons do not seem as energized or enthused since his departure. The need to move forward seems more of a task and a challenge for the congregation and leadership. The positive things that were experienced when Pastor Allen was leader have somewhat been dissolved. The direction of the congregation seems a little uncertain. Leadership seems to be focused on the church calling a pastor. The question for me is, do Vine members want a leader? Or do they want to lead themselves? My fear is that Vine will lose its stability, slip back into its old ways of doing things, and give up the idea of becoming an outreach church. There is fear that Vine might face a power struggle among the leaders. The Word of God says, "How can they hear unless there be a preacher and how can they preach, unless they be sent?"

As a former Interim Pastor of Good Shepherd Lutheran Church in Detroit, Michigan for six years and Good Shepherd Lutheran Church in Southampton, Pennsylvania, for one year, I understand clearly the power struggles among leaders when the church is in interim mode. The important things such as making disciples, spiritual growth, development, and maintaining the daily operations of the church tend to be pushed aside. Rather, who is in charge in some instances becomes more important than who has been communed and how many disciples have come to Christ on Christian experience, by letter, or by baptism. Counseling, pastoral care, and the concerns of the sick and shut in could be at risk. Vine's new resolve to reach out to lapsed and prospective new members could go unaddressed and become no longer important.

Value of the Project for Ministry of the Church

The value of the project for the ministry of the church has made the congregation aware of its shortcomings and its need to be more loving and inclusive to those who take the time to visit and worship with Vine. The project has challenged the ministry of the church to look at how it does ministry and how effective the ministry is relative to the concerns and challenges facing Vine Memorial. The project has been valuable in that it has encouraged the ministry to look at its outreach and mission and come to understand new, more effective ways to do outreach and mission. The project has shown leadership the importance of training, workshops, self-reflection, self-awareness, and education along with implementation.

Spiritual formation and contemplative prayer have been tools the project has made available to the ministry of the church. Nothing should be attempted without prayer and reflection. The importance of teamwork has been emphasized throughout the project. Planning, preparing, and organizing have motivated the ministry of the church. The impact and power of the witness of preaching has been favorable. The need for the congregation to welcome lapsed and prospective new members to Vine and to make disciples for Christ has been made primary. As Cleophus Larue affirms,

An all-powerful God continues to be a precious attribute for a majority of those who constitute the African American faith community, and there is no doubt in their minds that this mighty sovereign is able to save. The God of the black church is conceived by the black religious tradition as being a responsive personal being with unquestioned, and unlimited, absolute power.[15.]

The value of the project to the ministry of the church has called for the church to stretch out and to reach beyond our comfort zones. Reach out to Lapsed and Prospective New members. Reach out in ways that are very important to bring them on board. It is paramount that Vine be intentional and consistent in reaching out to the community, to be creative, and to have an awareness that draws people to come experience the love of Christ Jesus. We must provide various ministries so that the race is not over before we begin. Therefore, Vine must continue reaching and stretching out to all humankind.

Just as Anderson and Coyner said, like the runner stretches when he is warming up for the race, so we too must stretch out as we "warm up" to the lapsed and prospective new members. We must create an environment of kindness. This kindness must be present during the worship experience. We must be mindful of the language we use. This will be helpful to a good worship experience for those who are visiting with Vine. It is important for language to be understandable and not use "churchy" words so that the worship experience can be easier for the newcomers to comprehend God.

Effective preachers are gifted people, but the gifts needed for good and faithful preaching are different from those of the electrifying speaker or charismatic entertainer. Faithful preaching requires such gifts as sensitivity to human need, a discerning eye for the connections between faith and life, an ear attuned to hearing the voice of Scripture, compassion, a growing personal faith, and the courage to tell the truth. These are gifts of the Spirit, and although gifts of the Spirit cannot be taught in the classroom, they can be named, developed, encouraged, shaped, and given direction and focus.[16.]

There must be an atmosphere of kindness and warmth that will not stem from leadership but will exist because it is engrained in the deep fiber and core values of Vine Memorial Baptist Church. However, this fiber and these core values require laying a strong foundation that intentionally develops individuals, processes, and teamwork to communicate to those who visit and worship with Vine. Moreover, this can only be done if Vine focuses upon God's love for everyone. The project for the ministry of Vine has laid a solid foundation

---

[15.] Cleophus J. Larue, *The Heart of Black Preaching* (Louisville, Kentucky: John Knox Press 2000), 5.
[16.] Long, *The Witness of Preaching*, 14.

to build spiritual growth and has given great insights into how to grow other ministries within the congregation as we seek to heal hurts and wounds among Vine, the leadership, and the community. This will create space for God to work and the Holy Spirit to convince, convict, and convert those who hear the Gospel of Jesus Christ and become disciples for Christ.

Insights into Ministry as a Consequence of Implementing the Project
When I began implementing the project, I discovered many things. Those who say they will support you and be with you are often the ones who leave you to stand all alone. At times, there was no one to talk to or listen to my doubts and fears. On occasion, I felt like giving up. Trust became an issue. Jealousy arose around me from those who saw and heard what I was doing. People I needed help from, and those who were in the position to get things done for me, pushed me to the side or did not carry out what I needed them to do. Commitment was not there from those I depended on. At times, I could not speak freely because I was fearful I would not be able to complete my project. During the Site Visit, I did not get the support from leadership I felt I should have gotten. Persons did not respond to invitations or did not participate in the Site Visit. Cooperation was not always given or received. Those who were supposed to set up the room or have materials available would not be present. Dates and times would conflict. People who were supposed to meet with me would not show up. Punctuality at times would be a problem for some people. I learned to pray more and trust God for what I was doing. I learned that God is faithful. Ministry is not easy—it requires a lot of time, prayer, planning, organizing, self-sacrifice, and reflection. Ministry is a call, and sometimes can be overwhelming. Sometimes I found myself asking the question, "God, where are you?"

Disagreements would arise, and I would need to resolve issues before I could continue doing the work that was required. Unexpected things would happen, and I would have to make adjustments, even though others were not willing to make the adjustments with me. Sometimes those who were in charge would not be prepared to carry out the assignment placed in their hands. Personalities would clash, and instead of focusing on the task before us, we had to deal with personality conflicts. Some days would be non-productive; although I had planned well, nothing got done. I learned how to pray and trust God for every situation, no matter how small or how big the concern. I learned to have a plan B if what was planned did not work out. I learned to both micro- and macro-manage.

I took time to learn personalities and identify the gifts and skills of those around me in order to get the best out of every participant for the ministry involved in the project. I took time to learn who people are, how they think, how they work, and how they interact. I learned personalities, whether intro-verted or extroverted. I learned which people were morning people and which were night people. I learned everyone may not be as dedicated as me. I learned that some people are always late, and that there are those who will give great ideas, but are poor planners and will not do anything. I learned ministry is not for everyone, and not everyone understands ministry. Ministry is complex; it is not just preaching. Ministry can burn you out, and you must have a wellness plan in place that includes exercise, rest, and eating healthy.

Ministry is not about the person doing the ministry, but about the needs of families, individuals, communities, congregations, leaders, the lost, and the homeless. It involves methodology, process, and implementation. Ministry is about addressing injustice, poverty, and other social issues, iden-tifying problems, and resolving them for the greater good of all. Ministry is about preparation, experience, reason, justice, and scripture. The greatest thing I have learned about ministry is people want to know if you can help them. Can they trust you, and can they build a relationship? Relationship, I learned, is essential to it all. From the beginning of the project, my goal was to build trust, be understanding, and have compassion. Those with whom I had a relationship were faithful, punctual, and would do anything they thought I needed or wanted done.

It is my belief that a good relationship can fix any problem, generate good conversation, and provide solid feedback. Strong relationships energize, en-thuse, and get people excited to do the work. Relationship creates fresh new ideas and moves people beyond their comfort zones, allowing them to plan, organize, strategize, and prepare well. Relationship helps people to become strong thinkers and make things happen. It provides peace when things could have gotten out of control. Relationship is the element that keeps balance among the many diverse thinkers and personalities. When I taught high school, I wanted to test the blessing I know relationship can be. So, one day I came in and I said, "Today we have to get a lot done. And we need to trust one another in order to accomplish what has been set before us today." I divided the class into two groups. I chose a leader for each group. It was the leader's job to blindfold one individual in the group.

The leader, along with the rest of the group members, had the task of getting the blindfolded person from one side of the room to the other side without incident. The leaders and group members could not touch the person, but could only give instructions—turn left, go straight, or turn right—until the blindfolded person got to the other side of the room.

I learned that until I trust you, until you trust me, until we trust one another and God, anything that is impossible will remain impossible. When I trust you, when you trust me, and when we trust God, everything impossible will become possible. Among the greatest things I have learned while implementing this project is that I must trust God. The songwriter says it this way:

I've had many tears and sorrows, I've had questions for tomorrow, there's been times I didn't know right from wrong.

But in every situation, God gave me blessed consolation that my trials come to only make me strong. Through it all, through it all, I've learned to trust in Jesus, I've learned to trust in God.

Through it all, through it all, I've learned to depend upon His Word.

I've been to lots of places, I've seen a lot of faces, there's been times I felt so all alone.

But in my lonely hours, yes, those precious lonely hours, Jesus lets me know that I was His own.

Through it all, through it all, I've learned to trust in Jesus, I've learned to trust in God.[17]

During the project, this small group exercise I had done as a high school teacher created such a blessing for me and all those who took part. I along with the students learned the power of trusting God and one another. The blindfold forced the group members to lean on the other persons. The power and victory to accomplish lay in depending on the other group members who could see from the one side of the room to the other side. The power rested in knowing that without the instructions of the other members of the group, the blindfolded person would be unable to get to the other side of the room

---

[17.] *Lead Me, Guide Me: The African American Catholic Hymnal* (Chicago, Illinois: GIA Publications, Inc., 1987), p. 228.

without depending on the other teammates. The need to see through the eyes of the other group members was the victory to get from one side of the room to the other side of the room. The need to bond with the other group members was the faith needed to do what the blindfolded person could not do. The need to listen to the specific instructions that each group member gave was the will to get to the other side of the room and be free of the blindfold. Getting to the other side of the room would only be possible with the help of all the other group members.

Trust is the greatest asset I have gained from implementing the project for ministry. I have learned to trust God. Through this process, He has removed doubt, discouragement, and the fear of not accomplishing what He has called me to do at Vine Memorial Baptist Church. Trust God when you do not know how things will work out. Trust God when those you are working with are not seemingly with you. Listen to the specific directions God gives to you. Even when the blindfold is on, trust God.

Bond with God, and know that He has done it in the past, and He will do it now. Trust in God is important. It moves God to speak to you, and it leads God to guide and direct you. It allows God to get you from one side of the room to the other side. Depend on God and know God will open the pathway to accomplishment and achievement in Him. Your dependency on God will activate God's power on your behalf. God's eyes will become your eyes, and even when you are blindfolded, you can get from one side of the room to the other side. Trust God, and it will activate God's faith that is your faith, as well as activating God's specific instructions for your life, for your ministry, and for your call.

"Trust in the Lord with all thy heart and lean not on your own understanding. In all your ways submit to him and he will make your paths straight" (Proverbs 3: 5-6, NIV). A call to ministry requires one to trust God, and ministry also requires we trust the God in one another. In ministry, we must rely on others for support and strength. We need others to share what they have done and how it has worked for them. Trusting others is healthy for having a successful, effective ministry. Trusting others is important for establishing healthy relationships as well as building strong, lasting, productive ministries and making disciples for Christ.

Project Concerns and Opportunities in the Community

The concerns and opportunities in the community are great. Vine Memorial Baptist Church is located on the west side of Philadelphia. It is a lower- to lower-middle class section of the city. The crime (including murder) and high school dropout rates are high. Vine does not offer programs that are needed to raise the self-esteem and self-awareness that is so desperately needed among our youth. There is a recreation center located in the area that allows for the young people to play basketball inside and outside, and there is a swimming pool. There is a small neighborhood library located in the area which does not get much use from our youth and offers no programs that could address their concerns. There is a need for after-school tutoring, parenting classes for young mothers, and mentoring programs for young fathers, as well as family counseling for substance abuse and domestic violence for parents and youth alike. Programs like these would help to change the negative identity of our youth and neighborhood.

The Library and the Recreation Center could work in a joint effort with Vine Memorial Baptist Church to combat the high crime and murder rate and the high dropout rate among our youth in West Philadelphia. Joint projects with the Library could include:

- After-school programs to educate both youth and parents
- Parenting classes
- GED programs for high school dropouts
- Computer skills training that would involve young millennials from the community in tutoring others
- Career Day—professionals in the community could share insights into their careers
- College/Trade School Night—representatives from admissions and financial aid departments of area schools present information for youth and parents
- Employment center
- Tutoring and homework center

Joint projects at the Recreation Center could include:

- A local neighborhood police precinct where retired officers provide education and training about crime and violence

- A Junior Cadet program, in which youth are hired to run errands for the elderly, and develop healthy relationships between community and police officers
- Swim classes for all ages
- Sewing and cooking classes and sports programs that would involve volunteers from the community

Programs such as these would allow Vine to develop relationships with those who live in the community and assist in decreasing escalating high school dropout and high crime rates. This approach of teamwork would change the identity of our youth and our neighborhoods. Joint programs would lay the groundwork for developing relationships and trust and provide the help that our youth and families need. We would see the power of teamwork and trust. We would see ministry forming and shaping a positive identity within the neighborhood. Crime, poverty, and education would be transformed into a positive life changing experience for Vine and the community. Not only will human conditions change, but spiritual and moral growth will take place within the community, which is the call of Vine and the work of the ministry. Instead of people having no perspective or a bad perspective of Vine, the community and leadership will be working together in harmony.

The community will become an active part of Vine. Instead of Vine driving the community away, Vine should draw the community, show love as well as embrace all people and not just those who are connected to the founder and organizers of the church. This will happen when Vine listen to the narratives and stories of the community and understand how the stories of the community connect with their story. Vine must respect and value the stories of those who are a part of the neighborhood. Vine Memorial must be aware that their story and the story of the community is woven into the big story of Jesus Christ. Our stories connect us one with another through the love of Jesus Christ for all humankind. The concerns of the community become opportunities to grow together in ministry, to love one another as Christ loves us, and to unite the community and Vine as one body in Christ. What comes to mind is the story told by an old pastor during his sermon. The pastor's sermon text was the 23rd Psalm:

The Lord is my shepherd, I lack nothing. He makes me lie down in green pastures, he leads me besides quiet waters he refreshes my soul. He guides me along the right paths for his name's sake. Even though I walk through the darkest valley, I will fear no evil, for you are with me; your rod and your staff, they comfort me. You prepare a table before me in the presence of my enemies. You anoint my head with oil; my cup overflows. Surely your goodness and love will follow me all the days of my life, and I will dwell in the house of the Lord forever. (NIV)

The pastor began with this story:

There was an old man who was a herdsman. He and his grandson were together out on the farm herding the sheep. The man began to tell his grandson about the work of a herdsman and how he handles the sheep. The man said to his grandson, "Love your sheep, and take care of your sheep. Feed your sheep and give them the best of care."

Later that week the grandson and his grandfather boarded a plane and headed to Scotland. The first place the grandfather took his grandson was to a farm where they could see some sheep. As they watched the herdsman taking care of the sheep, they saw the herdsman giving the sheep the best of care, loving them and feeding them. As they continued to watch, they saw a second herdsman interact with another group of sheep. He began to hit them, yell at them, and hit them even harder. Soon the boy said to the grandfather, "Grandfather, I thought you said a shepherd takes good care of his sheep, loves them and feeds them." The grandfather paused and then said, "Grandson, what I did not tell you was there are two kinds of shepherds—shepherds; that draw their sheep and shepherds that drive their sheep. That's a shepherd that drives his sheep."

The work of ministry is to draw the community together, to give the community the best of care by loving them and meeting their needs. Ministry will draw the community to Vine, empower the community, change the negative identity of the community, and make disciples for Christ. When ministry does not feed the community, or meet the physical and spiritual needs of the community, then the ministry is driving the community. What kind of ministry are you providing, Vine? Is your ministry drawing the community or is your ministry driving the community? The work of ministry should draw communities and transform negative conditions and broken neighborhoods. With the teamwork of all parties, positive work can take place.

31

Congregation and Community Transformation
as a Result of Project Implementation

Vine has to be educated and made well aware of the need to be more welcoming to the community. Some improvement has been made. As a direct result of the project and the gospel preaching a small number of people from the community have become candidates for baptism. The identity of the community has not changed much regarding the attitudes towards Vine and the high crime and high school dropout rates. There is still a great deal of work that the community, church leadership, and congregation must do to live in harmony and make disciples for Christ. Awareness, implementation, and education have been modeled. From these teachings, Vine is in a good position to spiritually grow, multiply in number and re-imagine its ministry for leadership, the congregation, and the community.

CHAPTER 3

Findings and Practices for Ministry

Appendix L contains the information provided in the interviews. Participants expressed that church was a part of their lives as children and young adults and shared how once they got older, they stopped attending church. Some got married and then stopped going to church. Participants shared that once they stopped attending church for a period of time, they felt the need to participate again in the life of the church. Their coming back to the church stemmed from the experience of being raised in the church, and the power of the gospel message and preaching kept an inner connection to God and the church. The participants talked about how their parents sang in the choir, taught in Sunday school, and served as Deacons and Deaconesses. They connected to the church because attending church was a great part of their rearing, serving God and having relationship with the congregation. Connecting to the preaching was also important to those who participated in the project. Connecting to the preaching was effective for the participants when the preacher did not specifically preach to any individual, but included him/herself and the whole congregation in the sermon. Sermons that talked about faith and encouraged the listeners to be strong in the Lord were helpful in drawing those who heard the sermon. This type of preaching made those who listened to the sermon accept their errors and sins, move to be more obedient to the teachings and principles of God, and be more participatory in church.

Participants shared the importance of the pastors attending seminary, being called and trained to effectively lead, preach, and serve the people. When this is not the path a servant leader takes, this makes it more difficult to hear the message of God. This also impacts the creativity of preaching. In today's world training is important for servant leaders to be effective in delivering the message of Jesus Christ. Gardner Taylor affirms, "To seek and find God's movement in human affairs and to cry out, passionately pointing to where that stirring is discernible though scarcely ever indisputable is the preacher's task."[18.]

According to the participants, how the preacher approaches a person is important, too. It is important that the preacher does not use the sermon to talk at a person. The preacher should be conversational as he/she proclaims the gospel of Jesus Christ. If this is not done when talking to lapsed members or prospective new members, the opportunity to draw them to Christ and to Vine could be lost. Approach is important and could also determine if you come back to visit. Growing up in church has been helpful as well. As one participant stated:

> *It provided the opportunity for me to see the joy my grandparents had when they went to worship. That joy did not stay at the church my grandparents brought this joy home to us. Now that my grandparents who were servants and leaders in the church are with the Lord, their faith has influenced me and my family to continue worshipping and praising the Lord.*

It is the preaching of the gospel message, parents, grandparents, and guardians who have influenced the relationships that many of the participants have grown to love about God and the church. It is circumstances, difficulties in life, personal failures, failed dreams, lost jobs and opportunities, failed marriages, drug-addicted family members, as well as the faithfulness of Jesus Christ that have brought me back into the church. It is my desire to live with Christ now and forever that drives me to continue in Christ Jesus, even when I want to give up. It is the preaching of the true and living Word of God that sustains me. In I Corinthians 9:16b, Paul says, "For the necessity is laid upon me, yea woe is unto me, if I preach not the gospel!" The Apostle meant that the righteous requisite that rested upon him was that of a forceful and sincere witness

---

18. Gardner Taylor, *How Shall They Preach?* (Elgin, Illinois: Progressive Baptist Publishing, 1977), 38.

to Jesus Christ as the Lord of life and Son of God, even to the point of giving up his life. Amos Jones declares:

> *When the Black preacher answers the call, he hears the same kind of unilateral requirement. It must be remembered that Martin Luther King, Jr., was a Baptist preacher and he gave his life for what he preached. Preaching and what he preached was, as Dr. Charles G. Adams of the Hartford Memorial Baptist Church of Detroit, Michigan once said, not an option but an obligation.*[19]

Another project participant shared something a preacher had once told her. When this preacher was a child, at one time, she didn't want to go to church, but her parents told her, "You are going to go to church as long as you live in our home."

So her parents made her go to church. After a while, the young lady loved going to church. She said, "Where would I be if my parents did not make me go to church and learn about God and listen to the preacher share the gospel of Jesus Christ?"

The preacher believed she would have gone to jail or be dead. James Harris stated:

> *The sermon is not only able to cut out the mess that exists in the lives of folk who flock to hear the word, but in doing so, it heals the wounds of those who have been hurt by the painful blows of life. The sermon is more than a salve, or topical ointment; it is a transforming instrument a scalpel, a sword, indeed, a two-edged sword that cuts in both directions so that it gets to the heart of the matter, penetrating to the core where the essence of one's life is affected and where hope can be restored, rejuvenated, and rekindled.*[20]

On another occasion, a project participant shared the importance of hearing the good news of Jesus Christ because it soothes and gives hope and protection in time of trouble. The young man shared how he was raised up in the church,

---

[19] Amos Jones, Jr., *As You Go, Preach: Dynamics of Sermon Building and Preaching in the Black Church* (Nashville, Tennessee: Bethlehem Book Publishers, 1996), 26.
[20] James Henry Harris, *The Word Made Plain: The Power and Promise of Preaching* (Minneapolis, Minnesota: Fortress Press, 2004), 127-128.

got married, moved into a new home with his wife and children. One day, he was at work and his wife and children were asleep. The home was just built, and the alarm system was scheduled to be installed the next day. A robber broke into their home while his family was asleep. His family was not harmed, and only a few items were taken. The insurance company replaced the stolen items. But God protected his wife and children while they were asleep. For him, the good news of the gospel can serve as protection. In this instance, the preaching was positive and spoke to his life situation.

Those participants who were not raised up in the church but who attended church on special occasions talked about how meaningful the sermons were. They talked about their experience on the way home and how the sermons continued to be in their hearts. They talked about how the sermons encouraged them to become more active in the life of the church. The sermons were the most important part of the worship celebration. They told how the sermons moved them from a feeling of emptiness to a desire to hear more about the power of the Holy Spirit that comes through the power of preaching and more about how the Holy Spirit dwells within us. They talked about the conviction they felt knowing the power of the Word of God, and how unsettled they felt when they were not consistent in worship or serving God. They spoke of the needed blessings that could only be experienced in worship and through hearing the preached Word of God. Some asked for prayer that they would yield to the will of God for their lives and become a part of the church, not just on holidays or special occasions, but as full and active members in loving relationship with Vine and in full relationship with Jesus Christ.

The pastors who were interviewed by the Local Advisory Committee gave fresh insights into how preaching might impact outreach to newcomers and lapsed members. Preaching to anyone, particularly to lapsed and prospective new members, requires the pastor to empathize with the hurts and pains of those who sit in the pews seeking a Word through the power of preaching. The pastor must be careful as he/she chooses language and words to strengthen, encourage, and empower the listeners. The preacher must be sensitive and careful to include the situations of each person listening to the message. The power of language is important to the listener because the misinterpretation of a word can negatively affect how the listener hears or doesn't hear the preached Word of God and could result in the listener not coming back to visit. It could also impact how the listener is transformed or not transformed by the message. It is equally important for the preacher to be as careful about what he/she is saying as what he/she is not saying. According to James Harris:

> The language of the African American preacher, a language that extols freedom, justice, repentance, and salvation, is similarly multi-voiced. It's often the language of the scriptural text as well as the language of the people and their contexts. It is a language of life and death, faith and hope. It is a language of freedom while yet struggling to be free. This language that Martin Luther King Jr. spoke in his speeches and sermons. It was a language that captured my spirit and spoke to my heart and soul. It was the language of Henry David Thoreau, Paul Tillich, Karl Barth, and Reinhold Niebuhr, as well as the language of Deacon Jones and Aunt Jane. It was the language that fused the experience of the Black church and the white academy.[21.]

The delivery style is important to the listener as well. Are you talking to the listener through the preached Word of God or are you talking "at" the listener? To talk "at" the listener will be interpreted as rude and arrogant, and the listener could easily be turned off from the message or see the preacher and preaching in a negative light. Through the preached Word, the preacher must convey the love of God and Jesus Christ and the fact that Christ died for the sins of the whole world, including the listener. The preacher should use illustrations and words to reach the heart of the listener through the preaching of the Word of God.

The preacher should be cordial to the visitor and take initiative to make the visitor feel personally connected and welcome to the church. The preacher should be warm in his/her handshake and greeting and greet the visitor with a warm, sincere smile. The preacher should introduce him/herself, have small talk with the visitor and say, "God loves you and so do I. Welcome! And do come to visit again." The preacher should not be aggressive as he/she approaches the visitor, but instead be gentle, passionate, kind, and loving. When the preacher speaks to the visitor he/she should talk "to" the visitor, not "at" the visitor. The preacher's conversation should include something that con-

---

[21.] Harris, *The Word Made Plain*, 53.

nects him/her to the visitor or to the church or to his/her personal narrative and story, as Wimberly suggests:

> *These narratives suggest ways to motivate people to action, help them to see themselves in a new light, help them recognize new resources, enable them to channel behavior in constructive ways, sustain them in crises, bring healing and reconciliation in relationships, heal the scars of memories, and provide guidance when direction is needed.*[22.]

The preacher must know that all persons have value and must approach the visitor with this spirit and understanding. The value is not just human, but all persons have spiritual worth as well. This makes them available to Christ Jesus and Vine Memorial. Their spiritual value will allow them to be used by God and to use their gifts to uplift Vine and the community, witnessing as disciples for Christ. The preacher should attempt to tap into the human and spiritual worth of the visitor in conversation, or in written correspondence with the visitor after he or she has visited the church. Through surveys, visitors may be assisted in discovering their specific gifts and areas of interest for ministry. It is also important for the visitor to see and know the power of the Holy Spirit that lives in the preacher, because by the spirit the visitor evaluates the authenticity, transparency, and love that is present in the preacher. When the visitor can discern the Holy Spirit in the preacher's life, there is the opportunity for relationship to develop between the church, the visitor, and Jesus Christ, and also increase the preacher's ability to transform the visitor through the power of the Holy Spirit and preaching.

In this way, visitors become warm and receptive to the preaching of the Word of God. This is made possible in part because the goal of preaching is to speak to the life issues of the hearers, seeking to connect them to the transforming power of the gospel message. The sermon should be simple, clear, and relevant to the life situations of those who hear. Questionnaires and surveys are helpful in determining the effectiveness of the sermon: What did you relate to that you heard in the preaching of God's Word? How did the preached Word of God move you to be different and better as a person? What did you do to be better and different? Questions such as these also help the preacher to better

---

[22.] Edward P. Wimberley, *African American Pastoral Care* (Nashville, Tennessee: Abington Press, 1991), 12.

know the needs of those who are present in the worship/preaching experience. Because those who are visiting come with burdens and concerns, the final questions to ask are, "What are your physical and spiritual needs? What are you expecting from the preached Word of God for your life?" The need for God in the lives of those who hear the preached Word of God is important to those who visit and hear the Word of God. People who are seeking God want to know how God can help them, how they can trust God, and how they can develop a relationship with God. This is the door the gospel message can open for those who are seeking relationship with God. While the preacher helps to open that door through delivering the gospel message, the ultimate provision God provides through the gospel message is salvation for all who believe, obey, love, and serve Him.

The message of Jesus Christ must be one of inclusion that requires pastors, preachers and leaders to have an indwelling spirit of compassion for all people. For it is God's will that none should perish. If we only have a heart of love for those we serve, commune with, and lead, we will be in danger of limiting our ministry of service and leadership. If we feel differently toward those who are a part of our ministry and congregation, we are not exercising the spirit of inclusion for all people. We are being partial, and the Word of God says, "God is not a God of partiality" (Romans 2:11). So, if God is not a partial God, how can we as leaders serve only those who are a part of our ministry and congregation? Would this please God? Are these the statutes, promises, commandments, and teachings of Jesus? If we as pastors and leaders limit our ministry to those within the church, how can we gain lapsed members and prospective new members into the church and invite them to be in relationship with Christ Jesus? No, we should not feel one way toward those who are not a part of our ministry and congregation and another way toward persons who are. Jesus said, "I come that *all* might have life and have it more abundantly" (John 10:10).

The witness of preaching is powerful and must be done in love when preaching to all people. The good news about God must be presented both to those who are members of the congregation and those who are lapsed or prospective new members. Yes, when the gospel is proclaimed, as pastors and preachers we must inform all who listen about the consequences and judgment that comes from God when we sin and disobey the will of God. This judgment comes only from God, through the Scriptures and from the preacher through the preached Word of God.

Proclaim the message; be persistent whether the time is favorable or unfavorable; convince, rebuke, and encourage, with the utmost patience in teaching. For the time is coming when people will not put up with sound doctrine, but having itching ears, they will accumulate for themselves teachers to suit their own desires, and will turn away to myths. As for you, always be sober, endure suffering, do the work of an evangelist, carry out your ministry fully. (II Timothy 4: 2-5)

As the preacher prepares and presents the preached Word of God, he/she must be mindful to present both the judgment of God and the grace and love God has for all people. Tell how God is a God of judgment, but also share how God is a God of grace when we repent of our acts of sin. The Bible says, "If we say we have no sins we deceive ourselves, but if we confess our sins; God who is faithful and just will forgive our sins and cleanse us from all unrighteousness" (I John 1:9).

The aim of the preacher and the entire congregation, members and visitors alike, is to build relationship between the lapsed members and perspective new members. The importance of building relations is to develop trust, a trust that will allow dialogue between the preacher, preached word and prospective members to invite them to Christ Jesus and to become an active part of the congregation, using their God-given gifts and talents to build up others and to spiritually mature in faith and in God's grace. Through this relationship, new members will develop trust to empower them to grow as they live out the precepts, statutes, promises, and commandments of Christ Jesus and experience the power of the Holy Spirit and saving power of Jesus Christ. They will come to know the work of the church, the role the church has in our lives, families, and the community in which we live, and will feel welcomed, loved, respected, appreciated, and valued.

There are various reasons Vine has not been able to bring back lapsed members, according to the project interviews. Not all reasons are to do with Vine. Some participants have indicated life circumstances, such as moving out of the home and no longer having parents to encourage and demand church attendance, divorce, broken homes, and back-sliding situations. Others have said that they made a personal choice to no longer attend church on a regular basis because of work and family responsibilities. Yet many have said that they still yearn to be a part of the life of the church that has guided most of their young adult and adult lives. The need for church fellowship, guidance, wholeness, and peace has been almost impossible to ignore. Many have said the church has been a part of their growing up, which leads me to understand the power of the Scripture that says, "Raise up a child in the way he/she will go and when they get old they will not depart from it" (Proverbs 22:6). Many participants have spoken of the pain and frustration not attending church has caused them. Several have talked about how the preaching of the gospel message, along with their parents, grandparents, and guardians, have demonstrated the power of assembling together with the church and the love they have for the church even though they are not active members. These statements lead me to believe that there is hope for these lapsed members, for Vine, and for the church universal—hope to grow spiritually, to multiply in number, and to make disciples for Christ.

According to my project research, preaching was not a reason lapsed and perspective new members did not participate and worship at Vine. It is the power of the gospel message to grow the church and make disciples for Christ. Therefore, the gospel message must be simple and clear. The message must speak to the issues concerning all who hear the message of Jesus Christ. The preacher must be personal with those who visit and experience the gospel message. The sermon should not talk at those who are listening to the message, but should speak hope.

The gospel message must include language that speaks to and resonates with the listeners. The gospel message must speak in a way that the power of the Holy Spirit is activated. Spiritual transformation, change in identity should be present in the lives of those who hear the gospel message. The gospel message should inform the listener of the danger of sin, disobedience to God, and God's judgment. The message should tell of the grace and love of Jesus Christ. The gospel message should be inclusive of all people. The preached Word of God should challenge the listener to be of a contrast (different than the world) community. The message should be inspiring, energizing, and should empower the listener to move beyond his/her present circumstances and conditions and live free from the slavery of sin.

According to Johnny B. Hill:

> *What the church doesn't talk about is acted out in the pews and the*
> *pulpit. And talk without intervention too quickly turns into gossip*

which guarantees that many worshippers will leave church serv-
ices week after week with the same issues and problems of life as
when they entered. We're at a point in the life of the local church
that demands we begin to take an active role in confronting the
elephants in the room. Historically the church has successfully ig-
nored domestic violence, denied alcoholism and drug addiction,
justified adultery, demonized human sexuality, blamed
HIV/AIDS and down-low-ism on the homosexual and bisexual
population, and turned its head away from blatant fornication
among heterosexuals.[23.]

Vine Memorial has become comfortable with not dealing with issues that face the church. Membership growth and tithes and offerings are low to non-existing. Those who are not connected to the organizers and founders of the church are rejected, run out of the church, and leadership is not held accountable. And the church goes on as if all is well. Hill continues,

If we really believe that the local church is a hospital for the sick, then we
should not be surprised when sick people show up. Some show up with hyper-
tension, some show up blind, some show up in need of spiritual development,
and some show up with emotional frailties and psychological disorders. Some
people are difficult, manipulative, jealous, rebellious, and mean. Others ap-
pear anxious, or depressed, or their speech is scattered and incoherent.[24.]

Vine can train leaders through workshops using in-house persons who have leadership skills and training or use outside trained persons to address the concerns regarding leadership issues. Leadership training will assist the congregation in welcoming lapsed members back into Vine, inviting new members to Vine and to Christ Jesus, and addressing other concerns and issues facing the church.

It is my belief more can be understood about Vine through its church history, a history built by organizers who had a family church philosophy. While this way of thinking had its pros, it also excluded those who were not connected to family members of the organizers and founder. It has been the aim

---

[23.] Johnny B. Hill, *Multidimensional Ministry for Today's Black Family* (Valley Forge, Pennsylvania: Judson Press, 2007), 14.
[24.] Ibid., 23.

of the project to address the need for the church to be healthy, to be able to meet the needs of all members of the congregation and community of faith.

> *Therefore, if there is any consolation in Christ, if any comfort of love, if any fellowship of the spirit, if any affection and mercy, fulfill my joy by being like-minded, having the same love, being of one accord, of one mind. Let nothing be done through selfish ambition or conceit, but in lowliness of mind; let each esteem others better than himself. Let each of you look out not only for his own interests, but also for the interests of others.* (Philippians 2:1-4, NKJV)

Church leaders must teach the principles of Jesus, which are love, humility, and servanthood, to the entire congregation and community, so that these principles can be applied to creating strong and healthy relationships with one another. It is through knowledge, positive loving attitudes, values, and relationship skills that we will provide the environment for healthy relationships between Vine Memorial Baptist Church leadership, the congregation, the community, and lapsed and prospective new members. Showing love, we can destroy the many things that stop us from having strong loving relationships with each other. Additional suggestions the project aimed to introduce include:

- Christian Education
- Awareness
- Commitment
- Forgiveness
- Unity
- Relationship Building
- Teamwork
- Trust
- Getting to know the community

The project further suggested only the Christian education sessions should include talking about Jesus, and that this should be done in a non-intimidating way. All the other conversations should answer the questions, "Can you help me? Can I trust you? Can we build relationship?"

43

Christian education must serve as a primary tool for preparing leadership, the congregation and the community for the work and service of the Lord. The teachings must be insightful and empowering. Christian education must be presented in a way that all persons can relate. The teachings must be simple, clear, and relative to all people. Christian education must address the needs and concerns of the leaders, congregation, and the community. Christian education must be the foundation upon which to build healthy leadership, a healthy congregation and a healthy community. Christian education principles must include the teachings, statutes, promises, commandments, and precepts of Jesus Christ, the foremost being love. Christian education must address sin. It must address obedience to Christ, the judgment of Christ, the Salvation of Christ, and the Grace of Christ. Soundly grounded in these understandings and teachings of Christ, the church can get back to the true work of making disciples for Christ. As a result, the church promotes awareness, education, and implementation.

I have observed at Vine, over the years and during implementation of the project, that persons are sometimes stereotyped by perceptions that are held by those who have been a part of the church at large for years and by those who are connected to the organizers and founders of Vine. These attitudes and ideas often marginalize visitors and prospective new members, preventing them from having full acceptance of leadership and disallowing their complete participation in the life of the church. These attitudes also inhibit spiritual growth and identity transformation from taking place. And those who come to church leave the same way they came—having made no new connections and leaving the visitors disappointed and disconnected.

Earlier in the project report, I stressed the need for the community, Vine, retired professionals and high achieving students who are a part of Vine to come together as a team, to work in harmony to lower the high crime and high school dropout rates as well as meet many other community needs. Vine must make available all its resources to the community and seek to obtain more. Vine must embrace the holistic view, which means to embrace the concerns of the community as a part of ministry and not see the community and its concerns as separate from the work of ministry.

The church has the opportunity and obligation to develop creative strategies and methods for supporting, affirming, and empowering the community so none would perish. This will provide greatly for wholeness and healing among leadership, the congregation, individuals, families, and the community. This is directly related to the ministry of Jesus and, therefore, is the ministry of the church. If we strengthen leadership, the congregation, and the community through planning and developing, we enrich the faith and spiritual journey of believers, and we bear witness to God's goodness in the world in which we are called to live out our faith. Elizabeth Johnson outlines this process in two steps. The first step involves two things:

- Identify the ministry leadership
- Provide education

The second step involves five things:

- Gather the community to evoke the power of God to discern the nature of the programs
- Develop resources and implement programs that arise during the discerning process
- Network with other church and community programs
- Access programs
- Explore funding options if necessary[25]

> *The spirit of the Sovereign Lord is on me, because the Lord has anointed me to preach good news to the poor. He has sent me to bind up the brokenhearted, to proclaim freedom for the captives and release from darkness for the prisoners, to proclaim the year of the Lord's favor and the day of vengeance of our God, to comfort all who mourn, and provide for those who grieve in Zion to bestow on them a crown of beauty instead of ashes, the oil of gladness instead of mourning, and a garment of praise instead of a spirit of despair.* (Isaiah 61:1-3, NIV)

Motivation for Other Ministry Contexts

All through Jesus' ministry, He practiced hospitality. Jesus' aim was to include all people. As a result, Jesus had a spirit of hospitality. He loved on all people no matter what—Jew or Gentile, Protestant or Catholic, Baptist or Methodist.

---

[25] Elizabeth Johnson Walker, in Hill, *Multidimensional Ministry for Today's Black Family*, 91.

Jesus showed love. It was *agape* love, an unconditional love, a love that require nothing from us, but a love God has naturally for all his created and creation. It is a love that is pure and genuine, a love greater than anything one could ever experience. This same love, Jesus requires all of us to show toward one another. And Jesus says, "By this all will know we are His children, if we have love one for the other" (John 13:35).

In Romans 12:9-13, Paul says:

> *Let love be genuine; hate what is evil, hold fast to what is good; love one another with brotherly affection; outdo one another in showing honor. Never flag in zeal, be aglow with the Spirit; serve the Lord. Rejoice in your hope, be patient in tribulation, be constant in prayer. Contribute to the needs of the saints, practice hospitality.*

When Job was protesting against his sickness, one of the virtues he claimed was that he never neglected hospitality. In 31:32, he said, "The sojourner has not lodged in the street; I have opened my doors to the wayfarer." Gordon Fee expounds: .

> *Humility and mutual regard must characterize relationships among Christians, with believers exercising their varied gifts to support the functioning of the church, the "body" of Christ. Sincere love, abhorrence of evil, mutual devotions and respect, diligence in service, joy, perseverance, prayer, charitable support of fellow Christians, and hospitality comprise the particulars of Paul's prescription for relationships within the church. Toward non-Christians, even persecutors, believers must demonstrate a forgiving spirit, empathy, sympathy, non-vindictiveness, even hospitality, so that good gets the upper hand. Leaving vengeance to God prevents the Christian from being consumed by evil.*[26]

Humility is very important for Vine bringing transforming identity among leaders and the congregation. The community is primary in building and sustaining spiritual growth and positive relations between the leaders, the congregation and the community of faith.

---

[26] Gordon D. Fee & Robert L. Hubbard Jr., *The Eerdmans Companion to the Bible* (Grand Rapids Michigan: Eerdmans Publishing Co., 2011), 649.

Another motivation for ministry observed through the project was outreach. When and if effective outreach is modeled, it will be a pathway to healing the ills among leadership, the congregation and the community. Effective outreach will also be a path that will lead to Vine reconnecting with lapsed members, welcoming newcomers to Vine, and making disciples for Jesus Christ. It is a commission to grow the body of Christ in a healthy way, rather than merely for the sake of a number. A number should not be the goal of Vine or the church universal. The goal of outreach is to bring more souls into the Kingdom, into a healthy body. The body of Christ is a growing body. Jesus repeats this idea in Acts 1:8: "You will receive power when the Holy Spirit has come upon you, and you will be my witnesses." He is commissioning the saints to multiply (to grow the body of Christ). Jeffrey Miller clarifies:

> *William Temple said, "The church is the only cooperative society in the world that exists for the benefit of its nonmembers." As a local body of Christ (a church, a people of God), one of our highest callings is to exist for the benefit of our nonmembers. We must communicate the message of salvation and be witnesses among them— salt and light (Matt 5:13-15) in a dark and decaying world—so that people will populate the Kingdom of Heaven ultimately, and will populate the body of Christ today.[27.]*

It is, therefore, our commission from God to be a witness to a dark, dying world. Our witness must be a message of salvation so that those who do not know the Lord can come to know Him in a more excellent way. The message of salvation is not only for those who are connected to family members, organizers and founders of Vine or any local church. But the opportunity is available to all who will come to hear and believe Jesus Christ. This includes lapsed members, prospective new members, and anybody from the community of faith. It is through effective outreach that we grow the church spiritually and multiply the body in number. Jesus said,

> *Go ye therefore, into all nations, baptizing them in the name of the Father and of the Son and of the Holy Spirit teaching them to*

[27.] Jeffrey E. Miller, "Growing the Body of Christ," *The Body of Christ Series*, https://bible.org/series-page/5-outreach-growing-body-christ (accessed November 21, 2016).

observe all things whatsoever I have commanded you and lo I am with
you always even unto the end of the world. (Matthew 28:19-20)

Translated from Greek to English, it would read this way:

Going therefore disciple ye all the nations, baptizing them in the
name of the Father and of the Son and of the Holy Spirit, teaching
them to observe all things whatever I gave command to you; and
behold I with you am all the days until the completion of the age.[28]

The great commission God gave is the work of the local church (Vine) and the church universal. It is the work of all leaders and pastors, it is the work of the congregation, and it is the work of the community. A narrow heart excludes many. Including only those who are connected to organizers and founders must not be the core value of Vine for effective ministry and spiritual growth. The work of the ministry must not be separated from the concerns of Vine leadership, the congregation, and the community, but must be addressed as a part of the ministry to include all who are available to Christ Jesus.

Therefore, the Great Commission involves not only evangelism and leading people to baptism but also nurturing believers and training them to share their faith after they become mature disciples of Jesus and in turn are prepared to lead others into discipleship with Christ. The Great Commission's focus means to multiply the disciples.[29]

The ministry of the church (Vine) must be modeled, motivated, and implemented in the love of Christ. Ministry must be centered in the heart of the cross: the cross where Jesus died for all humankind; the cross that redeems, convicts, convinces, and converts all of us from our past sins and ushers us into new mercies and new grace every day; the cross where the sins of the world were carried by Jesus, who was without sin but came to the world in human form to model suffering and claim victory over sin and Satan. This was sin that separated us from God, that motived us to be disobedient to God, and that was overcome by the blood of Jesus Christ and resurrection from the grave. Vine must stand as the pillar in the community, both for those who

---

[28] Alfred Marshall, *The Interlinear NASB NIV Parallel New Testament in Greek And English* (Grand Rapids, Michigan: Zondervan Publishing House, 1993), 99.
[29] Michael Dornbrack, "The Discipleship Challenge," *Ministry: International Journal for Pastors* (May 2016), accessed November 16, 2016.

know God through the pardon of their sins and for those who don't know Christ through the pardon of their sins. Vine must serve all people, love all people, be a witness to all people, and see the transforming power in the lives of all people. Through the power of the Holy Spirit, we can see change in leadership, in the congregation, in the identity of the community, and in those who are not connected to Vine, Jesus Christ and the community of faith.

Where Is Vine Memorial Baptist Church in All of This?

If Vine is going to experience increased cohesion, understanding, spiritual maturity, and membership growth, Vine has to be more aggressive, innovative, relevant, and progressive in its community outreach. Vine has to engage in the healing of conflicts among leadership, among the congregation, and among the community.

Outcomes of the project will include continuous Christian education, education about the community and neighborhood, awareness, intentionality, and prayer. A committee will be in place to continue to address and solve problems and concerns that arise among leadership, the congregation, and the community. Healthy dialogue among leaders, congregation, and community will continue. We will continue the sharing of narratives and stories of all people and will seek out the gifts, talents and desires to serve among the community. The congregation as well as leadership will develop and grow in partnership with the community. Training will take place, and we will learn effective ways to be inclusive of the community and those who are different. The ultimate goal will be to multiply discipleship, leadership, and the congregation and to transform the identity of the community.

Where Does Vine Go from Here?

Vine Memorial Baptist Church still has a distance to travel before it can see the desired spiritual transformation, identity change and unity it seeks among leadership, the congregation, and the community of faith. Vine can build on the progress put in place from the work of the project. Christian education must continue to be taught to leadership, to the congregation, and to the community. Leaders, the congregation, and the community must be aware of the differences that divide the unity and harmony God set out through ministry. Vine must continue implementing spiritual core values as it works to minister to all people. Vine must be intentional and serious about the race to reach out, connecting lapsed members and new members to Vine and to Jesus Christ. Vine must continue to hold onto the many benefits it has provided the congregation, leadership, and community.

Vine must begin to re-imagine who it can become. Vine must begin to pull together its resources to decrease crime and high school dropout rates, to tutor students, and to connect to outside services and sources to bring jobs, training and education to the community. Vine must be more open to all people and see the gifts that God has given to all humankind. Vine must be more loving and forgiving of its past and the past of others and have a spirit of inclusion, not just for those who are connected to the organizers and founders, but to whosoever will. Vine must continue to celebrate those who serve and achieve among the congregation, but also begin to celebrate the community, the work, and the progress it achieves. Examples include: celebrating a single parent who has achieved his/her high school diploma; celebrating a parent who has been free of drugs for any amount of time; celebrating a man or woman who has been expunged from the penal system; and celebrating a couple who has been living outside of holy matrimony but is now married.

The congregation cannot expect the pastor or a few ministries or a few congregants to do the work. The work is dependent on the entire church— the pastor, lay leaders, and the congregation. It is a team effort that requires all ministries working together as God ordained it to be. Vine must know the immediate response that is necessary when newcomers or lapsed members visit Vine. Just as when we are running a race, quickness is crucial. When visitors attend Vine, we must contact them immediately.

In the wisdom of Douglas T. Anderson and Michael J. Coyner, authors of the book titled, *The Race to Reach Out*: timing matters. It is my strong belief too; that Vine must know timing is vital in connecting newcomers, lapsed members to Christ and the church. Using Anderson and Coyner's metaphor of a race, as a runner runs, he or she is very aware of the importance of turns on the track. So also, Vine needs to be aware that it is important not to fight the turns on the track course, but to flow smoothly into the turns. This will allow the runner (Vine) to sustain balance and speed. This is equally important in making disciples, connecting lapsed members, and inviting new members to Christ. Vine needs to be flexible to changes, keep in stride, and yet be aware of the changes that come unexpectedly, making the adjustments that are required without delay in the process as we make disciples for Christ and the church.

Vine must stay mindful of the importance of handing off the baton smoothly, without disruption or dropping the baton. This is a necessary skill in making the race successful. It is, therefore, required of the church to be in contact with the visitors and get important information about the physical and spiritual needs, interests, gifts, talents, and desires of the newcomers. This will be helpful in connecting them to Vine and Christ. Consistent practice is necessary for the ministries, leaders, and the entire Vine team to be successful in bringing newcomers and lapsed members to Vine, connecting them to others, and making disciples for Christ. Vine must be the primary runner in the race to reach out to newcomers and lapsed members for Christ. Vine must endure to the end. We can't give up or stop running the race. We must exercise daily, stay prayed up, stay in tune with the concerns that face leadership, the congregation, the community, and stay prayerful for the physical and spiritual needs of leadership, the congregation and the community. We must depend on the power of the Holy Spirit to transform leadership, the congregation and the community. Scripture tell us, "The race is not given to the swift or the fastest, but to those that endure to the end" (Ecclesiastes 9:11). Endurance means to be strong, to hold up, to hold out, to sustain and to be sustained. Endurance is also important to making disciples and making a difference in lives and in the world today. Vine must invest in those who are not connected to the organizers and founders of the church.

CONCLUSION

Vine through its history has made great contributions to leadership, the congregation, and the community. Down through history, Vine has fallen into some unhealthy paths that have grown out of its past. Although Vine's intent is not to be unhealthy, over time, it has fallen into the hurts, pains, and brokenness of the early church. As in the history of the Early Jerusalem Church, things were not always done right. People were excluded, and the church did not always stand up to defend and affirm, to rebuke and correct evil, or to confront racism, sexism, injustice, mistreatment, and exclusion. The church at times seemed to hide her head in the sand, not standing up for the poor, the brokenhearted, the downtrodden, the marginalized, and those who have no voice.

The church has turned many away and left some with many questions for God. For some, this was enough to leave the church and even turn away from God, wondering if God existed or if God was real. The church has made its mistakes and had its failures, but the church continues to reform to meet the needs of the people, set the standards for Christian living, and serve as a refuge for the lost. Although 30-plus years ago, the church was the number one influence, today the church does not rank at all. Instead, culture rules. Jesus is hidden in culture and denied by many.

Yet, God is still the Groom, and the church is still the Bride. Jesus said, "Upon this rock I will build my church and the gates of hell will not prevail against it" (Matthew 16; 18). It is through this assurance that I take new hope in the church. It is in this declaration from Jesus that I still depend on the power that is in the church. This same hope keeps me reimagining a healthy future ministry context for Vine Memorial Baptist Church: to carry out the ministry and principles of God's Word in leadership, among the congregation, and in the community; to make disciples for Jesus Christ until He comes back to rapture the church and all who would hear the preaching of the Gospel message of Jesus Christ; and to welcome all and whosoever will.

Vine must continue to model, mentor, and find fresh insights to decrease high crime and high school dropout rates and meet the physical and spiritual needs of all people. We must make the community a place where all people can live, work and serve God, the church, and the community and experience a new Heaven and a new Earth that displays the love of God. We must share in the diversity that God has given all humankind for the betterment of all people. Jesus in his ministry was diverse. When he talked to farmers, he used farmer language, and when he talked to sinners, he used parables (earthly stories with heavenly meanings). The preached gospel message must continue to be powerful and at the center of the worship experience, making disciples for Christ. The gospel must be simple, clear, and must speak to the situations of all people who hear the word of God. Vine must be intentional and deliberate when lapsed members and prospective new members are in attendance:

- Get the necessary information needed to stay in contact.
- Provide surveys that ask questions about the gospel message and how it touched them.
- Develop relationships with all visitors that answer the questions: "Can you help me? Can I trust you? Can we have a relationship?"
- Learn the spiritual and physical needs of each person who visits or joins Vine.
- Discern each person's spiritual gifts and talents. Know the ministry desires of all persons and direct them to the ministry they desire and are called to.
- Provide Christian education and leadership training.

Vine must continue to train, nurture, and multiply disciples for Christ. Vine must expect leadership, the congregation, and the community to continue to spiritually grow and to reimagine, model, and mentor the "what is," looking to the future ministry of Vine and the "what is to come."

APPENDIX A

DMIN LOCAL ADVISORY COMMITTEE
PERSPECTIVE MEMBERS INVITATION

Reverend Clinton Craig Hoggard
8400 Lindbergh Blvd. Suite 717
Philadelphia, Pennsylvania 19153-1510
Cell: 267-593-4865

January 5, 2016

Dear Doctor of Ministry Local Advisory Committee Member:
It is with thanksgiving, joy and anticipation. I invite you to become a part of Reverend Clinton Craig Hoggard Doctor of Ministry degree project. The goal of the project is to answer the question, "How to bring lapsed members back into Vine Memorial Baptist Church, and welcome new members into Vine"? Is there a connection/relationship between preaching as a result of lapsed members and new members not becoming a part of Vine or is it something else?

Therefore, I ask you to accept the invitation and commit to the time table, strategy and plan we must put together beginning January 13, 2016, to successfully complete the DMIN project. Projected dates and times the Local Advisory Committee will meet will begin Wednesday January 13th, 2016, 1:30pm-3:00pm 659 56th Street, Annex Building.

The group meet each week at the Vine Memorial Baptist Church location Wednesday 1:30pm-3:00pm to strategize, and develop Doctor of Ministry project for implementation around the question. How do we bring lapsed members back into Vine, and welcome new members into Vine Memorial Baptist Church?

After conducting the audio interview recordings, the data and responses will be analyzed by the team and a written summary will give findings and conclusions and recommendations from the data provided by the participating groups.

Please begin strategizing narrative questions to ask the participants around the topic question to Saturday March 5, 2016 for 1.5 hours. Upon completing the project, we must meet for a follow up to assess our outcomes and findings, and make recommendations.

Reverend Dr. Kevin D. Miller Director of Theological Admissions Drew Theological Seminary, June 28, 2016 Site Visit.

TIME LINE FOR DMIN PROJECT

October – November: Prospectus is approved. Reverend Dr. Kevin D. Miller/Drew Theological Seminary

December – January: Local Advisory Committee Meet to develop plan to implement project, agree on method (How we do it). Examples: Surveys, narrative questions for pastors and unchurched groups.

February – April: (Planning, organizing and strategizing and implementing project).

April – May: Follow up – Local Advisory Committee/meet to assess, measure project outcomes. June 28, 2016.

APPENDIX B

DMIN PROSPECTUS LOCAL ADVISORY COMMITTEE ROSTER

Please Print Clearly

1. Email _____
    Cell # _____

2. Email _____
    Cell # _____

3. Email _____
    Cell # _____

4. Email _____
    Cell # _____

5. Email _____
    Cell # _____

6. Email _____
    Cell # _____

APPENDIX C

**DMIN PROGRAM DREW UNIVERSITY MANUAL
LOCAL ADVISORY COMMITTEE TRAINING**

I. _____ PROJECT PHASE PP. 34-38

II. _____ SAMPLE PRELEMINARY PP. 47-49

III. _____ DMIN PROJECT PROSPECTUS PP. 62-75

IV. _____ PROJECT IMPLEMENTATION & WRITING PP. 119-123

V. _____ REVIEW SITE FORMS DATE: _____
LAC MEMBER: _____

APPENDIX D

DMIN THANK YOU INVITATION SYMPOSIUM OF PASTORS

Dear Pastor:

March 8, 2016

Thank you for accepting to participate in Reverend Clinton Craig Hoggard's Doctor of Ministry project. The project will seek to answer the question. How do we preach the good news of God to African American unchurched persons? The hypothesis seeks to discover if there is a connection between the preacher, preaching, the good news, and members of the church as a result of African Americans living unchurched lives? Or is there some other cause(s)?

There will be 10 questions asked and audio recorded around the above named topic and hypothesis.

The data you share; will be used only for the purpose of the DMIN project and writing. Your name, identity, will be kept confidential and secure at all times. You will sign two consent forms, one for your and my records.

Local Advisory Committee members present that day will be Deacon William Bryant, (will time keep), Deaconess Jackie Right (audio recorder), Reverend Clinton Craig Hoggard, DMIN Candidate (will prompt questions).

You are invited to attend the audio recording interview, Monday March 21, 2016, @ 11am-12:30pm, Second Mount Zion Baptist Church conference room, 3814 Parrish Philadelphia, 19104. After interpreting the audio recording; the recording will be erased and destroyed.

A special thank you to Reverend Dr. James Moore for serving as Host Pastor; opening up his facilities and church for the use of continued ministry and service to God, to us, and to the community.

Reverend Hoggard invited all participants to the lower unit fellowship hall for dinner and fellowship.

Again, thank you for your commitment and support as colleagues and so-journers, servants and leaders for Christ Jesus.

Reverend Clinton Craig Hoggard

APPENDIX E

DMIN SYMPOSIUM OF PASTORS QUESTIONS

MARCH 21, 2016

1. When you preach the good news of God; what do you say about God to the unchurched?

2. How do you respond to the unchurched who attend your church? How do you greet them? What do you say to them?

3. Are you verbally aggressive or passive? Do you talk to the unchurched or do you talk at unchurched persons?

4. Do you seek the human/spiritual worth value of the unchurched who visit your church? If so, how? If not, why not?

5. How do the unchurched respond to you as pastor/servant/leader? Do they see the spirit of God in you? If so, how do they see the spirit of God living in you? If not, why do they not see the spirit of God living in you?

6. How do the unchurched respond to your preaching/good news about God? What impacts them to respond this way to preaching the good news about God?

7. Do the unchurched who visit your church see a need for God in their lives? If so, why? If not, why not?

8. Do you feel a particular way toward the unchurched than you do about persons who are members of your congregation?

9. How do you present the good news about God to the unchurched? Do you present the good news about God in a judgmental way to the unchurched? Or do you present the good news of God in a judgmental way and share God's grace to the unchurched?

10. Why is it important to build relationship with the unchurched? How do you build relationship with the unchurched? And how do you sustain relationship with the unchurched?

APPENDIX F

DMIN PASTORS PARTICIPANTS GROUP 1

Will meet Monday March 28, 2016 659@West 56th Street, Philadelphia, PA. 19131. 11am-1pm. The audio interview recording will be used to gather data for Doctor of Ministry project and dissertation writing.

APPENDIX G

DMIN PARTICIPANTS GROUP # 2

Will meet Saturday March 19, 2016@659 West 56th Street Philadelphia, PA. 19131. 12noon-1pm. The audio interview recording will be used to gather data for Doctor of Ministry project and dissertation writing.

APPENDIX H

**DOCTOR OF MINISTRY PARTICIPANTS
THANK YOU AND INVITATION FORM**

March 5, 2016

Hello participant's let me first say thank you for accepting the opportunity to take part in my research project for the degree of Doctor of Ministry, and for taking time out of your schedules today for orientation.

It is a pleasure to have you for orientation. I thank you for your commitment to participate in a small group setting, audio recording.

In your folders, you will find your group date, time and location to meet for the audio recording.

Saturday March 12, 2016. 12noon-1pm group one will participate in the small group audio recording. 659 West 56th Street, Philadelphia, PA 19131.

Saturday, March 19, 2016, 12noon-1pm, group two will participate in a small group audio recording. 659 West 56th Street, Philadelphia, PA 19131.

Your participation will provide data for writing my Doctor of Ministry Dissertation. Title: "How do we preach the good news of God to African American unchurched Persons"?

There are two groups of unchurched persons. One those persons who attend church on occasion, two those persons who do not attend at all.

Today you will sign two consent forms, one for you and the other for my documentation. Your identity and information will be kept private and will be used only for the use of the project.

Again, thank you for your participation in the research project. Your responses are valued, so please be open, and honest in your response(s) to all questions. Thank you!

APPENDIX I

DOCTOR OF MINISTRY CONSENT FORM

You are invited to be a participant in a research study about, "How do we bring back lapsed members into Vine Memorial Baptist Church, and welcome new members into Vine?" The study seeks to discover; is there a connection/relationship between preaching as a result of not bringing back lapsed members into Vine Memorial, and welcoming new members into Vine? Or is there some other reason(s)? You were selected as a possible participant because Reverend Hoggard and the Local Advisory Committee members reached out to you through family and friends of Vine Memorial Baptist Church where we worship and I serve as an Associate Minister. We ask that you read this document and ask any questions you may have before agreeing to be in the study. The study is being conducted by Drew University Theological Seminary. Reverend Hoggard, is a candidate for Doctor of Ministry degree program.

The purpose of this study and research questions is to receive data from participants that will assist in answering the question is there a connection/relationship between preaching as a result of Vine not bringing lapsed members back into Vine Memorial, and welcoming new members into Vine? Author L. Bond conducted a study on 21st Century Legends of African American preaching. African American Preachers to include: The late Gardener C. Taylor, late Sam Proctor, James Forbes and Henry Mitchell. Bonds wrote out of the thought. Most whites believe all black preaching is the same. Bonds disputes this claim when comparing, contrasting and analyzing the preaching of Taylor, Proctor, Forbes and Mitchell.

Bonds, gives us a close up look at the men otherwise you would not have gotten if you did not hear them. Bonds highlighted the many similarities the Legends share. All of the men have individual distinctions. The thread with Bonds research for me is. Bonds links the power of preaching not just with our African American worship experience, but links preaching with our African American History and African American experience. This has always been the wealth and richness of African American preaching. Preaching the good news about God; serve as a vehicle of strength and hope for African Americans even today.

The length of time for the audio recording for the two distinct groups will be for 1 hour. Group one will consist of lapsed members. Group two will be composed of perspective new members. There will be 5 persons in group one and 5 persons in group two. Each group will be interviewed at separate times and ten questions will be asked and participants are asked to respond to the questions.

You can respond to any question. If there is a question you do not want to answer; you do not have to respond to it. When one person is speaking please allow him/her to finish speaking before another person speaks. You can end participation in the audio recording at any time without consequences. This study has no risks to the reputation, physical, or mental well-being of participants. When all questions have been asked and answered, you can leave.

The records of the study are confidential. Your identity and data will be kept private, secure at all times and will only be used for the use of the Doctor of Ministry research project. The data will always be stored in a safe, secure place, accessible only to Reverend Hoggard, Deaconess Jackie Right and Deacon William Bryant.

After listening to the recordings to analyze, compare, contrast the collected data, all recordings will be erased, all written transcripts will be shredded and destroyed by the end of April. No information presented will risk your identity.

Your decision whether or not to participate in this research will not affect your relations with Drew University. If you decide to participate in this study, you are free to withdraw from the study at any time without affecting those relationships without consequences.

The participants will be debriefed of the purpose of their participation in the Doctor of Ministry research project. Participants will be informed the research project will be audio recorded for the purpose of Reverend Hoggard getting respondents statements accurate and correct when quoting respondents responses and for the purpose of analyzing, comparing, and contrasting the data.

The researchers conducting this study are Reverend Clinton C. Hoggard (Doctor of Ministry Candidate), Deacon William Bryant (Church Clerk), and Jackie Right (Deaconess). You may ask any questions you have right now. If you have questions later, you may contact the researchers at clint43hoggard@yahoo.com.

If you have questions or concerns regarding this study and would like to speak with someone other than the researcher(s), you may contact csavage@drew.edu.

The procedures of this study have been explained to me and my questions have been addressed. I understand that my participation is voluntary and that I may withdraw at any time without consequences. If I have any concerns about my experience in this study. Mistreated unfairly or felt unnecessarily threatened), I may contact the Chair of the Drew Institutional Review Board regarding my concerns.

Participant signature _____

Date _____

APPENDIX J

**DMIN PROJECT ORIENTATION
PARTICIPANTS ATTENDANCE FORM**

NAME: _____

DATE: _____

CELLULAR # _____

EMAIL ADDRESS _____

FACILITATOR: REVEREND CLINTON C. HOGGARD CELLULAR #
267-593-4865

APPENDIX K

DMIN PROJECT PARTICIPANTS DEMOGRAPHICS SURVEY
PLEASE PROVIDE THE FOLLOWING RESPONSES

1. AGE

2. GENDER

3. TYPE OF EMPLOYMENT

4. LEVEL OF EDUCATION

5. MARRIED

6. SINGLE

7. DIVORCED

8. SEPARATED

9. CHILDREN

10. NO CHILDREN

APPENDIX L

DMIN PROJECT QUESTIONS FOR
LAPSED NEW MEMBERS PARTICIPANTS

1. Was church part of your life as a child, young adult, and adult? If so, how? If not, why not?

2. Were your parents, guardians, or family, regular participants in church? If they were how did they participate in the church? If your parents, guardians, family, did not participate in the church why?

3. How do you relate to church? Is there a relationship with you and the church? How did you come to connect with the church? If not, why do you not attend church?

4. When and if you hear a preacher preaching how does or did that impact you in a positive or negative way? What was positive? What was not so pleasing, about the preacher or the preaching?

5. Share what experience(s), or who influenced your relationship to attend church? If you do not attend church share what experience(s) impact you not attending church?

6.   If you once attended church, but no longer attend church; what impact you choosing to no longer attend church?

7.   Do you see the church differently as a result of having once been involved in the life of the church?

8.   When you heard preaching about the good news of God, was it good news to you?

9.   When you go to church is preaching one of the reasons you attend church? If so, why? If not, why not?

10.   What will make the church more appealing to you to consider becoming part of the church?

APPENDIX M

EVANGELICAL CHURCH SHOPPING, EXPLAINED

Two-thirds of Americans who attend churches in evangelical denominations have looked for a new congregation (67%). According to the Pew Research Center, that's higher than any other US religious group (the national average: 49%). Pew asked 700 evangelicals why they wanted to leave their church and how their search went.

67%
OF EVANGELICALS HAVE LOOKED FOR A NEW CHURCH

WITHIN THE LAST 5 YEARS

16% 12% 39%
>10 YRS 5–10 YRS

THE REASON THEY WENT CHURCH SHOPPING (COULD SELECT MORE THAN ONE)

49% moved
18% disagreed with pastor
16% married/divorced
12% dissatisfaction with church or its theology
5% change in personal beliefs
3% distance/convenience
2% children's needs and education
2% wanted more community

HOW THEY SEARCHED

91% attended worship service
72% talked to friends or colleagues
71% talked to members of the congregation
64% talked to minister
36% looked for information online
18% called the new church

WHAT THEY WERE LOOKING FOR

94% quality of sermons
83% feeling welcomed by leaders
80% style of worship service
69% location
64% Sunday school for kids
49% having friends/family in congregation
49% volunteering opportunities
49% same denomination
47% different denomination

69% EASILY FOUND A NEW CHURCH. THEY CREDITED IT TO:

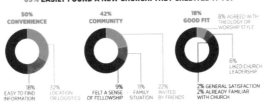

50% CONVENIENCE
42% COMMUNITY
18% GOOD FIT
8% AGREED WITH THEOLOGY OR WORSHIP STYLE
6% LIKED CHURCH LEADERSHIP

18% EASY TO FIND INFORMATION
32% LOCATION OR LOGISTICS
9% FELT A SENSE OF FELLOWSHIP
11% FAMILY SITUATION
22% INVITED BY FRIENDS
2% GENERAL SATISFACTION
2% ALREADY FAMILIAR WITH CHURCH

31% HAD DIFFICULTY FINDING A NEW CHURCH. THEY BLAMED IT ON:

43% bad fit   32% community   31% convenience

44% ATTEND MORE NOW THAN IN THE PAST. HERE'S WHY:

54% spiritual reasons
23% practical reasons
16% social reasons
8% other/no answer

15% NOW ATTEND LESS OFTEN THAN BEFORE. HERE'S WHY:

57% practical reasons
21% spiritual reasons
13% social reasons
8% other/no answer

BIBLIOGRAPHY

Aldred, Joe. *Preaching with Power: Sermons by Black Preachers*. London: Cassel, 1998.

Anderson, T. Douglas, and Michael J. Coyner. *The Race to Reach Out: Connecting Newcomers to Christ in a New Century*. Nashville, Tennessee: Abington Press, 2004.

Center for Biblical Leadership. *Spiritual Formation*. Cleveland, Tennessee: White Wing Publishing House, 1997.

Crawford, E. Evans. *The Hum: Call and Response in African American Preaching*. Nashville, Tennessee: Abington Press, 1995.

Dornback, Michael. "The Discipleship Challenge." *Ministry: International Journal for Pastors* 88, no.5 (May 2016): 6.

Fee, Gordon D., and Robert L. Hubbard, Jr. *Eerdmans Companion to the Bible*. Grand Rapids, MI: Eerdmans Publishing Company, 2011.

Harris, Henry James. *The Word Made Plain: The Power and Promise of Preaching*. Minneapolis, Minnesota: Fortress Press, 2004.

Hill, Johnny B. *Multidimensional Ministry for Today's Black Family*. Valley Forge, PA: Judson Press, 2007.

Jones, Amos. *As You Go, Preach: Dynamics of Sermon Building and Preaching In the Black Church*. Nashville, Tennessee: Bethlehem Book Publishers, 1996.

Larue, Cleophus. *The Heart of Black Preaching*. Louisville, KY: Westminster John Knox Press, 2000.

Lead Me, Guide Me, The African American Catholic Hymnal. Louisville, KY: GIA Publications, 1987.

Lischer, Richard, ed. *The Company of Preachers: Wisdom on Preaching, Augustine to The Present*. Grand Rapids, Michigan: William B. Eerdmans Publishing Company, 2002.

Long, Thomas G. *The Witness of Preaching*. Louisville, KY: Westminster John Knox Press, 2005.

Marshall, Alfred. *The Interlinear NASB-NIV Parallel New Testament in Greek and English*. Grand Rapids, MI: Zondervan Publishing House, 1993.

Miller, Jeffrey E. "Growing the Body of Christ," The Body of Christ Series. Last modified July 16, 2004. Accessed November 21, 2016. https://bible.org/seriespage/5-outreach-growing-body-christ

Mitchell, Henry H. *Black Preaching: The Recovery of a Powerful Art*. Nashville, Tennessee: Abington Press, 1990.

Obgonnaya, A. Okechukwu. *Precepts for Living, volume 19, 2016-2017*. Chicago, Illinois: Urban Ministries, Inc., 2016.

Shelley, Marshall. *Changing Lives Through Preaching and Worship*. Carol Stream, IL: Christianity Today, Inc., 1995.

Taylor, Gardner. *How Shall They Preach?* Elgin, Illinois: Progressive Baptist Publishing House, 1977.

Wimberly, Edward P. *African American Pastoral Care*. Nashville, Tennessee: Abington Press, 1991.

Wright, Tim. *Unfinished Evangelism: More Than Getting Them in the Door*. Minneapolis, MN: Augsburg Fortress Press, 1995.

CPSIA information can be obtained
at www.ICGtesting.com
Printed in the USA
BVHW022250250322
632294BV00001B/1